in grace,

Gene Cunning

# The # TRUTH IS AT # MY FRONT # DOOR

SPIRITUAL DIRECTION ON AGING BEAUTIFULLY

ILENE M. CUMMINGS

Copyright © 2016 Ilene M. Cummings.

All rights reserved. No part of this book may be used or reproduced by any means, graphic, electronic, or mechanical, including photocopying, recording, taping or by any information storage retrieval system without the written permission of the author except in the case of brief quotations embodied in critical articles and reviews.

Balboa Press books may be ordered through booksellers or by contacting:

Balboa Press
A Division of Hay House
1663 Liberty Drive
Bloomington, IN 47403
www.balboapress.com
1 (877) 407-4847

Because of the dynamic nature of the Internet, any web addresses or links contained in this book may have changed since publication and may no longer be valid. The views expressed in this work are solely those of the author and do not necessarily reflect the views of the publisher, and the publisher hereby disclaims any responsibility for them.

The author of this book does not dispense medical advice or prescribe the use of any technique as a form of treatment for physical, emotional, or medical problems without the advice of a physician, either directly or indirectly. The intent of the author is only to offer information of a general nature to help you in your quest for emotional and spiritual well-being. In the event you use any of the information in this book for yourself, which is your constitutional right, the author and the publisher assume no responsibility for your actions.

Any people depicted in stock imagery provided by Thinkstock are models, and such images are being used for illustrative purposes only.
Certain stock imagery © Thinkstock.

Print information available on the last page.

ISBN: 978-1-5043-6557-4 (sc)
ISBN: 978-1-5043-6558-1 (hc)
ISBN: 978-1-5043-6581-9 (e)

Library of Congress Control Number: 2016914637

Balboa Press rev. date: 12/08/2016

This book is dedicated to my mother and father.

Mission Statement

To inspire a national beauty conversation.

TABLE OF CONTENTS

The Truth is at My Front Door ix
Going Into the Room Empty xi
The Cardinal Rule xv
A prayer for guidance xvii

Part I.   Tell the Truth **1**
The Young Man on the Bus 3
The Lullaby of a Wisdom Teacher 8
Follow the Thread 13
Silence and Solitude 17

Part II.   Let Go **21**
Pockets 23
Forgiveness Helped Me to Let Go 34
The Older Woman and Her Young Man 41
Life Was Easier When They Were Small 47
The Powder-Blue Bathing Suit: Fear of Being Fabulous 52

Part III. Bring Meaning into Your Life **61**
The Pink Chrysler 63
This Is Where I Came to Heal 72
"For Your Age..." 76
Burying Yourself Alive Is a Distinct Option 80
The Spiritual Task of Meeting Yourself Fully 84

THE TRUTH IS AT MY FRONT DOOR

The truth is at my front door.

    I always knew she would call, but I'm not certain I want to let her in. Of course I want to age beautifully. I am told the first step in making this happen is to embrace the truth. Only I don't want to deal with this right now. The whole affair makes me uncomfortable.

    The truth brings an important message, but I'm not in the mood to listen. I make every excuse to avoid her. Yet here she is, at my front door. Should I embrace her, or do I keep ignoring her? I hear whisperings from other women that they are having problems with her too. Let's be honest; there is no one she won't eventually visit.

    I am told she brings gifts of wisdom, grace, and invisible forms of God. Some say she represents a beauty far exceeding anything found in a jar. I've been examining my face in the mirror more than usual, and every examination is taking on a life of its own. I don't feel good about this ritual, but I can't seem to stop. She knows about these things; that's why she is at my front door.

    I am told she wants to help me age beautifully. No doubt, she'll suggest I embrace the morning mirror and surrender to the face I see. Regardless of how determined I am to resist her message, she'll be triumphant in the end because the truth is always triumphant in the end. Admitting this makes it impossible to ignore her any longer.

    I gather my courage and open the door.

    She is standing there, looking me straight in the eye, and I wonder what I've been so afraid of. And no, she is not easy to look at! But she is the determining factor governing my ability to age beautifully. She carries a message, and here is what she says.

"Aging is not an object *out there*. Aging is an experience *in here*. You must learn to be in awe of it.

"And what do I mean by awe? Awe is the overwhelming feeling that something is out and about, breathing life into emptiness and exposing us to our best and highest selves. The awe of it all keeps us going and is the undergirding to a fresh approach to aging beautifully. Awe is that which pulls us deeper into our regenerating interior lives, where beauty can be felt, and grace has a chance to flourish. Awe brings sanity to everyday life by nudging our imagination and reminding us that we are creatures with gifts having nothing to do with calendar years. In a world gone crazy with unhealthy competition and a warped preoccupation with everything outside ourselves, awe lets in the fresh air of soul.

"You must not walk out on your life by abandoning who you are. You must not give up on your beauty because of aching joints, a face you no longer recognize, eyebrows that have disappeared, or lingering regrets about the road less traveled. You must not walk out on your life."

GOING INTO THE ROOM EMPTY

And so began my journey to discover how I could age beautifully.

I have witnessed older women who stood independent of their age. They went into the room empty every time. They were so *there,* displaying a sense of ease that was independent of the years they had lived. With or without the trappings of fashion, make-up, or ideas of being current, they personified presence. They lacked a need for approval from others and displayed an acceptance of themselves just as they were.

Over the years of thinking about aging and beauty, I came to define true beauty as the visible expression of having done our best to create a life based on telling the truth, being open to change, and choosing to live with meaning.

This book is for all women. Whether they are forty-five, sitting in a dingy kitchen wondering where their youth went; fifty-seven, living in a swanky Manhattan high-rise, looking in the mirror, and lamenting, "My God, what happened!"; a seventeen-year-old who wants to know about grace and grief and is unable to find women willing to mentor her on these topics; a popular seventy-five-year-old senior who is devastated when she goes to a party, and for the first time in her life nobody asks her to dance; or a self-confident, forty-nine-year-old professional who makes a six-figure income and can hold an audience of a thousand in the palm of her hand, but is terrified to speak about her upcoming birthday.

While each of these women is different, the truth will eventually be at their front doors too. Each will be tasked to tell the truth about the face and body changes that come with the passing of youth. It is the wise woman who works toward going into the room empty. She is the woman free of unhealthy outside noise, the influence of social constructs, and the forceful seduction to not tell the truth.

We need everyone's voice if we are to resist the craziness of having someone else decide what we should look like. It will be a liberating day when the insult coming from an antiaging cream modeled by a nineteen-year-old woman no longer fills our magazines. No one gains by this manipulation. The older woman is being hoodwinked, and the young woman does not get exposure to the honorable aging that would allow her to develop in sound ways.

We do not talk about our *experience* of aging. We talk about creams and lifts, how to prevent aging, avoid aging, circumvent and resist aging. We talk about fixing ourselves. It is time to feel comfortable with the words *aging* and *beauty* spoken in the same sentence as a natural coupling and to think of beauty as every woman's lodestar—something alive and throbbing with life.

A national beauty conversation, spoken from women's wisdom, is a subject we are ready to tackle. We do not have to march in the streets with our fists held high, rebellious and rowdy, demanding our right to age with passion, pride, and self-respect. We already have that right. What is needed is a common cause revolution that trumpets our honest voices. Voices that speak to the essential, individual expression of beauty personified by each of us.

The Truth is at My Front Door is not about bemoaning the loss of youth; it is about encouraging women to reach for the magnificent sweet notes still luring them toward a fully engaged life. Aging beautifully will never be the outcome of having achieved a worldly reputation, an unlined face, or money in the bank. It will be the outcome of laying claim to one's beauty rising from having lived an explored, expressed, and honest life.

For forty years, I have conducted women's groups and seminars throughout the United States. The women who left an indelible mark on me were those who took their place on earth seriously and embraced the inner work of personal growth. They were not superwomen. They were wonderful women doing the spiritual work of looking at themselves and taking responsibility for what they found.

Out of that healthy place, they were able to choose the kind of older women they wanted to become. The day they made the fundamental distinction between *choosing* their behavior as older women and *reacting* to the media's stunted view of older women was the day they walked into the room empty. They put down society's interpretation of being old and decided how they wanted to age. It led Lakshmi, a sixty-seven-year-old student, to exclaim with a broad smile, "I know my wrinkles are there, I just don't see them anymore." Lakshmi had walked into the room empty.

But let's be real. Aging does remind us of our vulnerability and finiteness, the dreams yet to be followed, the relationships still waiting for truth telling, and the tasks of accountability and forgiveness yet to be actualized. The Buddhist monk Pema Chrodon writes, "What we do accumulates; the future is the result of what we do right now." Ageless beauty will not magically show up. It is cultivated, practiced, and nurtured every day.

The cultural shaming associated with getting older has had horrible consequences. We have turned against ourselves, waged war with nature, and lied about how old we are. We disowned ourselves in a vain attempt to maintain an image we have outgrown. Until now, primary control of the beauty conversation has been yielded to media constructs that promote a view of aging and beauty that is inauthentic, unrealistic, and runs counter to all human progress. There is nothing wrong with wanting to look fit, healthy, and our very best. The importance of a wise exercise regime, a good skin care program, and a consistently healthy diet must be faithfully followed. And fashion need not be viewed as superficial. Fashion can be the legitimate expression of a woman owning the art of individuality.

At the end of the day, aging beautifully is always going to be about giving diligent attention to the ongoing process of personal growth. No woman can buy or exercise her way into protecting her beauty. The most brilliant body worker cannot do it for her. A truckload of broccoli and blueberries will not get her there either. Make no mistake about it: the greatest indicator of our ability to age beautifully is self-acceptance, and it will take a lot more than a fabulous face-lift to make that happen.

It is not necessary to be a tall, skinny woman committed to a fifty-dollar lip plumper. It is not essential to have a flat tummy, peerless skin, full eyebrows, someone in your bed at night, big breasts, big lips, a big vocabulary, a big personality, and a big paycheck. What *is* necessary are big thoughts about being beautiful and a determination to do the challenging and rewarding work required to fill the soul while living in a society that is doing everything possible to keep us from doing just that.

The beautiful older woman is a woman who is beautiful because she has established her beauty on her own terms and expresses herself in her own terms. She owns her power, her age, her earned wisdom, and yes, her sensuality. She flaunts her sensuality when it is appropriate to do so, but more than anything, she loves being a woman of beauty and grace and looks upon the sexist bigotry of contemporary society as a tragedy because it fails to recognize her as the force of the nature that she is.

THE CARDINAL RULE

Protecting your beauty is the cardinal rule for aging beautifully.

It is to make the clear decision to take care of yourself intellectually, physically, emotionally, and spiritually. How well you take care of yourself will determine how you experience the process of aging. With media images encouraging women to be someone other than they are, *protecting your beauty becomes political protest.*

Eventually, and in spite of great skin care, proper nutrition, vitamins, exercise, procedures, and surgeries, Mother Nature is going to have the final say. Societal norms pressuring women to preserve their youth at all costs runs counter to the healthy capacity to embrace life's journey. There is not a thing wrong with wanting to look our very best, but when we *depend* on preserving our youth in order to maintain a grip on reality, we are in serious trouble. Most of us want to age beautifully, but no one told us how. One thing is certain; it is not found at the cosmetics counter. It is found by accessing the spiritual power that has forged all progress from the beginning of time.

We call on our power when we choose not to give others the responsibility of deciding how we should experience our changing faces and bodies. I am all for exercising daily and eating correctly, but, by themselves, they do not go far enough. How well we protect our beauty will be measured by the peace we make with our own souls.

The following three principles offer spiritual direction:

1. *Tell the truth*
2. *Let go*
3. *Bring meaning into your life*

There is nothing simple about following these principles, but over time, they lead to aging beautifully. Trust the journey. Resist judging yourself and militate against keeping a running calculation of results. Aging beautifully is a *process* that will not be finished in a month or a year, but will take a lifetime. But being finished is not the goal. The goal is to protect your beauty as you nurture your beauty. Remain loyal to the principles underlying the cardinal rule. They will not betray you. Take comfort in knowing there will be tangible results both large and small throughout the journey. Although many gains will not be immediately apparent, they will show up over the long haul.

> *Aging beautifully is possible. However, it requires that you take responsibility for your own aging process. By accepting this challenge you will find yourself leaning into the spiritual life. The spiritual path requires that you embrace impermanence. Keep faith with the universe, commit to starting the journey, and trust the unevenness of the process. Please do not be overwhelmed by the size of the task that lay ahead.*

Remember, I was thinking of you as I sat writing late into the night, and every word of this book was meant to embrace you as you travel the path of aging beautifully.

A PRAYER FOR GUIDANCE

- *I pray I have the determination to stay the course when I get lost in the unevenness and uncertainty of the journey.*
- *I pray fear of the unknown does not overshadow my intuition, my goodness, and my common sense.*
- *I pray my inborn thrust to thrive will carry me beyond any identification with victimhood.*
- *I pray the night air of uncertainty turns to the silver moonlight of awe.*
- *I pray the deep beauty of my soul will be the master teacher leading the way.*
- *I pray discipline and patience become the undercurrent running through the days of protecting my beauty.*
- *I pray my choices will carry the echo of the millions of women who have gone before me, allies who trusted their wisdom to lead them home.*
- *I pray genuine honesty will be the wondrous outlet for letting go of fear of aging.*
- *I pray I have the courage to put one foot in front of the other as the portal of growth leads to transformation.*
- *I pray I find the spiritual maturation inherent in shining a light on the subject of aging beautifully to be the heroic act that heals my heart.*
- *I pray I find words of wisdom when supporting other women who want to embrace their beauty.*
- *I pray I can resist the negative media messages that fail to champion the older woman.*

Holy Spirit, hear my prayer.

PART I

TELL THE TRUTH

What is this faithful process of spirit and seed that touches empty ground and makes it rich again? Its greater workings I cannot claim to understand. But I know this: Whatever we set our days to might be the least of what we do, if we do not also understand that something is waiting for us to make ground for it, something that lingers near us, something that loves, something that waits for the right ground to be made so it can make its full presence known.

—*The Faithful Gardner*
Clarissa Pinkola Estes, PhD

THE YOUNG MAN ON THE BUS

Look ahead. You are not expected to complete the task. Neither are you permitted to lay it down.—Talmud

When I turned fifty-four I left everything that was humming along with ease to accept a job three thousand miles away about which I knew very little.

I received an offer to be the executive director of a newly established institute in San Francisco. The institute's goal was to help people discern the negative behavioral patterns of their parents and understand which, if any, of those patterns continues to influence their lives today. It was a beautiful program, and I jumped at the chance to start a new life. I was idealistic and unrealistically optimistic about making such a big move. My five children had all left home, and I was newly divorced after twenty-seven years of marriage. I didn't move because I was unhappy or because things weren't working in my life. On the contrary, things were working quite well. I rather loved being single and had no trouble finding handsome young men who were happy to romance an older woman, and my successful counseling practice showed every sign of growing. I moved because the evolutionary headwinds of California offered the opportunity to find out what else I had inside.

But things didn't go as planned. Although I started out with enthusiasm and optimism, these feelings quickly faded. The institute and its founder were not what I expected, but in all fairness, I had not yet learned that change of this magnitude required a period of adjustment and big-time letting go. Within a few months the glow of California turned to the heartache of regret. I had ruptured my sense of place, killing any idea that I was in charge of my fifty-four-year-old life.

The temptation to move back to New Jersey was enormous. I had been too cavalier about letting go of the things I had worked very hard to accomplish. A major triumph had been the purchase of a gorgeous three-story townhouse that I filled with white carpets, red velvet sofas, enormous green plants, white silk drapes, copper basins filled with ivy, and a cherry wood, four-poster, queen-size bed draped with eighteen yards of nylon toile lying atop its frame that sat nestled in a sunny loft bedroom. That house was more than a house. It was the place where I stopped ironing the dishtowels and began living like a movie star. My townhouse represented the dawn of self-hood, romance on a level I had never known, and freedom of choice I did not know existed.

I was leaving behind beloved East Coast friends that loved and supported me over a lifetime. It had taken many years to develop these relationships that I was now deliberately forsaking. This action still takes my breath away.

Long walks on the white, sandy beaches of South Jersey became memories punctuated with such longing that I had to stop myself from thinking about them. Afternoon trips into Manhattan with sojourns up Fifth Avenue wearing four-inch heels, treating myself to lunch at the Plaza Hotel, and loving the affirming whistles from the hard hats all haunted me. But I was restless. A distinctly rich period of my life had ended. The next step in the journey appeared, and though I could not be certain where it would lead, I asked the clarifying question, "What is important?"

To compound things, the executive position in San Francisco was not a good fit for my skills and gifts, and I resigned after fifteen very difficult, tearful months. By this time, the feeling of loss and regret filled my life. I loved San Francisco from the day I stepped off the plane, but its magnificent skyline never trumped the inquisition overtaking my thoughts: Had I made a big mistake? The shadow of grief followed me everywhere I went in my new city home, and there was nothing I could do but hope that given time, I could embrace my new life. I was in the throes of a complex set of emotions brought on by the loss of familiar, everyday activities, beloved friends, and patterns of behavior that lay behind in New Jersey. Had I understood that grief expressed is grief transformed, I would have fared better. It would be a long time before I understood that embracing one's grief is a powerful tool for the evolution of the personality.

But no, I could not admit that I was miserable; instead, I put on a happy face. After all, I was voted the girl with the greatest smile in my high school graduating class of 456 students. I knew how to look good so others would not be alarmed that I might have made a poor choice. And of course, I didn't want to make anyone uncomfortable.

I was somebody in New Jersey. In gorgeous, creative San Francisco I was starting from scratch. Several years would pass before I could admit, even to myself, that I was regretful of having made the move. I could not have foreseen the many marvelous people and deeply intense, creative, life-enhancing and fulfilling professional work that lay waiting for me to claim in California.

I even wondered if I had dislocated my life as a distraction from finally taking a good, hard look at myself. As a single woman relieved of thirty-three all-consuming years of hands-on mothering, I was most likely suffering from more than just a case of the empty nest syndrome. I was at the dawn of a new life cycle. It was brave to choose change at this level, and it was also very, very scary. I was closing one door and opening another without the slightest idea what I would find. I felt both joy and fear as new beginnings made their way through the corridors of my new life.

I felt like a trapeze artist deliberately letting go of the solid platform beneath my feet to fly through the air, suspended in time, with a trust that a new, solid platform would appear before me. Each time I reviewed why I moved, the answer was the same: I moved to California because something called me there. I simply had to go and would have regretted it all my life if I hadn't.

And then it happened. I was traveling to work on a very crowded 31 Balboa bus going to downtown San Francisco. All humanity was on the bus. Old, young, black, white, people with turbans, people tattooed with dragons and three inch Mohawks, people with purple hair, and people wearing black, three piece business suits. It was pure San Francisco, wildly diverse and wonderful! I loved the beauty of it all and was reminded of why I moved in the first place.

Then a clear voice was heard above the crowd. A young man wearing a crisp, white shirt and seated in the third row on the right side of the bus said to me, "Ma'am, would you like my seat?" Flustered, I quickly turned my head away.

Suddenly, losing my friends, my house, my network, and my changing role as mother paled in contrast with a feeling that I had lost something of even greater import. I had lost my youth.

It was many years before I told anyone about my encounter with the polite young man. He was after all that sensitive creature called a chivalrous male. His remark was really a gracious acknowledgement of me as a woman who had left behind a girlish persona and was exhibiting the social status of an older woman. But I heard and felt his comment as a personal assault of some kind. I heard and felt old.

His greeting rang in my head for years: "Ma'am."

The Wisdom Lesson

It is not enough to simply accept our age. Aging beautifully requires that we tell the truth about our age.

Every woman has a young-man-on-the-bus story. It is the first time you admit you are visibly aging and others can see it too. The antidote to experiencing an unhealthy reaction to this realization is to create a new reality. It is the red-nightgown reality.

In *Infinity in Your Hands*, Sandor McNab reminds us that nothing so determines who we will become so much as those things we chose to ignore. The point is, by ignoring we are aging, we create the very thing we are trying to hide. We show our fear in the set of our mouths, our posture, in our jealousy of the young, and in our reluctance to accept ourselves just the way we are.

By believing that our innate, essential life force is youth dependent, we arrive at the conclusion that we are not acceptable as we are.

My knee-jerk reaction to the polite young man made me realize I had lost something of immeasurable value. One word from the polite young man had the effect of stopping me dead in my tracks. I had not yet developed the graciousness to accept the fact that I was a woman who had begun to age, and it showed. I did not *feel* old, but I did not look like a young woman anymore. I looked like a middle-aged woman who looked good. I had not accepted the first law of aging beautifully: tell the truth. Therefore I failed to carry the bearing that shouts grace and self-acceptance. I was susceptible to outside forces reminding me that I was no longer young and my heart sank at the prospect.

There is a remedy for this situation.

Buy yourself the most luscious red nightgown you can find. Go to consignment shops, vintage boutiques, and thrift shops. Raid the attic, go through your best friend's closet, get out your J. Peterman catalog, and let everyone know you are a woman on a mission for a red nightgown. Take your time. This purchase is a manifesto. It does not matter if someone sees you in your red nightgown because someone else is not the point. The point is you are a beautiful babe. And beautiful babes can show up at any stage of life in a red nightgown. You have lived long enough, worked hard enough, and tried hard enough. Have your life, own your body, breathe deeply, and treat yourself to a cardinal moment. This has *nothing* to do with cellulite, soft bellies, age spots, wiggly arms, thin lips, or sagging breasts. You are on the earth to protect your beauty, raise the level of the beauty conversation, and learn how to take care of yourself.

Red nightgowns are *an experience.* They are *an event.* If it bothers you to look in the mirror while wearing your red nightgown, don't look in the mirror. Look in the mirror when you are ready. Be as good to yourself as you have been to everyone else. Just slither into bed and feel that nightgown doing its job of protecting your beauty. Let it help you slip into a dreamy self while you steadily recuperate from the world and its' poorly thought out ideas of what constitutes beauty.

Get together with other women and ask about their young-man-on-the-bus story. Ask each woman to explain the lesson inherent in the story. Ask what she would like to tell other women about the young man on the bus. Laugh and cry. Share the experience. Growing old is not the problem. The problem is we have made growing old the problem.

THE LULLABY OF A WISDOM TEACHER

Come. Come. Whoever you are. Wanderer, worshipper, lover of leaving. Come. This is not a caravan of despair. It doesn't matter if you have broken your vows a thousand times. Come. —Rumi

We are beautifully served when we have a wisdom teacher in our lives. She is the woman who is wise enough to know that it is wonderful to be young but knows with certainty that a woman makes a pack with the devil when she is dependent on *staying* young.

Dorothea was a teacher for me. Six feet tall and thick hipped, all eighty-four years of her were grand. Dorothea could never be called fashionable in her flowered crepe dresses and interesting felt hats. But she was definitely grand. Hers was a stately beauty coming from the core of who she was.

At the time, I was badly in need of a mentor and was blessed with finding Dorothea. I was moving from twenty-three years as a stay-home mother of five with a queen-of-the-kitchen identity to overnight accepting a job leading a newly created women's program at my local community college. I was in over my head from the start. I had no idea what it took to be a college administrator and failed to understand the titanic power of the women's movement sweeping the country. I knew about award-winning apple pies, raising babies, and I was a force to be reckoned with around a sewing machine. Oh, I knew what it was to work around the clock. Passion and physical stamina was never a problem. The problem was the enormous learning curve I had to master while the whole college community looked on. By the time I met Dorothea, I was a walking identity crisis.

I lacked any understanding that transformation on the level I had put into motion behaves like a wildly stressed, caged animal—frightened, confused, and unable to cope with the multilevel changes overwhelming its system. Having even a modicum of understanding about taking care of myself and having a support system would have made all the difference in my collapsing world. Nonetheless, a voice inside my brain kept screaming, "The time is now. Girl, hop aboard. The green light of a new dawn is leaving the station. No one knows where this is leading. But go you must!"

Increasingly, I had the feeling I did not know who I was. My husband and children did not know who I was, either. I was evolving from an unchallenged forty-four-year-old woman. I lacked all understanding of how big this shift in identity was. The flames of purgation were moving ahead, doing their job, burning away years of certainty and stability. The earth had moved under my feet, and there was no going back.

Everything was radically different, down to the clothes I wore and the food I ate. It was threatening and terrifying, and as I fell apart I wished I had not tampered with a life that had been humming ahead without threat. My children were young enough to still think I was cool, and as long as I did not disturb his life, my husband allowed me to do what I wanted. I fantasized all kinds of outrageous scenarios that would stop the momentum of my changing life, such as messing things up so badly in my new job that I would be fired and even trying to convince my New Jersey state trooper husband that we should move to New Hampshire on a fairytale concoction of living closer to nature. I wanted to go back to things as they were and looked for any excuse to pull into my shell where certainty could protect me. But the gears of change were in motion, and my destiny was taking shape before my eyes. The whole thing almost took me down. I kept putting one foot in front of another even as I seriously contemplated suicide.

Then I met Dorothea. The moment we met, I knew I needed her. What was most intimidating was that she wanted to know me! She saw something in me that I was yet to recognize in myself. The wisdom makers see beyond ordinary sight. They identify the starved soul, spot rudderless women, and gently step in to provide an anchor. I remember Dorothea saying, "You are a sensitive child; you must not let things hurt that sensitivity." That statement sounded like the beautiful lullaby I needed.

During the high art years of mothering, children took priority over everything. It never occurred to me there was life outside my pretty kitchen, church, the PTA, and the A&P. On a lark, I interviewed for a job to be the founding coordinator of a newly funded, noncredit woman's program at a community college twelve minutes from home. I had not even read Betty Friedan's classic, *The Feminine Mystic*. How ironic that I was tasked to lead a program that spoke to my own emerging self. It was 1975, and the air was electric with possibilities for women. Political signposts like Title IX and the ERA were making headlines, and though I failed to grasp the importance of these things, I was on my way to a life that had been touched by the fates. My kitchen with its checkered red and white curtains never had total pull on me again. Yes, there was something distinctly sad about it. But I was discovering a part of me that I never in my wildest dreams knew existed. It was clear, even to me, that this transition was about more than going into the job market. It was a spiritual call to rise to a new level of myself and take ownership of my whole self. There was to be no slow going, getting ready, testing the waters, or figuring it out. Time would have to make room for my sloppy transition that had come out of nowhere. My general feelings of stupidity about how things worked as a college administer almost killed me. But I kept going. Something essential wanted out.

As soon as the women's program was announced, women came to the campus in droves searching for that powerful place within. They came to be heard and to find a way to expand their lives without wreaking their lives in the process. Every woman was a new story being written right before my eyes. They were putting flesh on their dreams, and it was heaven to watch it happen. Initially, I ran the program on passion, intuition, hard work, and with the backing of two spectacular bosses, both who believed in me. They were mentors in every sense of the term. I owe them my career. The program succeeded beautifully. I had the advantage of not knowing how things were done. What I did know was what women wanted, and that was good enough for me! In time, I was singing them lullabies.

I often stood at my large office window and watched adult single women, mothers and grandmothers, take the terrifying step of enrolling in college. They were afraid of rocking the boat at home yet were drawn by the awe of forces gripping their souls. They were awakening to themselves as a work-of-art-in-progress, and in every woman I saw my own dreams were coming true. Forty-one years later, this six-year period stands out as the most rewarding of my entire career.

I don't remember when I first heard Dorothea say the words, "Be true to yourself." I only know that hearing them from a woman I respected made all the difference. She was a retired high school English teacher whose former students, themselves now retired, still drove down the Garden State Parkway from North Jersey to sit at her feet and listen to their old teacher talk about the things that matter. However wisdom was defined, everyone knew Dorothea had it, and we hoped by being in her fine company some of it would rub off on us.

Dorothea often said, "Well, dearie, we do the best we can, don't we?" I always heard that as a compassionate response to the things that can go terribly wrong. We did not worship her, but we loved sitting at the feet of a master. Dorothea was a wisdom teacher and never shied from accepting that role.

Growing old brought out a wonderful radicalness in Dorothea. Her interests were less about holding on and more about letting go. She moved forward on a current of subtraction, becoming a role model on how to age beautifully.

I lost touch with her after I left the East Coast but heard through the grapevine that she was seriously ill and living her final days in a dismal nursing home. I immediately placed a call. She was on a hunger strike and outraged that the staff was unwilling to follow her wishes. They poked and prodded and poured in nutrients, trying to extend her life. But in the end, she got her wish. I always loved her audacity; however, she brought it to the highest level while on death's door. Her staunch position left me with a deep respect for her capacity to remain true to herself even as she took her final bow.

It was pure Dorothea *doing the best she could*.

The Wisdom Lesson

Honest women prepare for their final journey. They pull on their truth and fortitude when it is time to let go.

Being true to yourself means having the courage to be loyal to your instincts and your feel for the world. You are special, and your inner resources make you unique.

Clarissa Pinkola Estes writes in *Women Who Run With the Wolves*, "Writers write and dancer's dance." The point is, if you are a writer who is not writing or a dancer who is not dancing, you are not being honest with yourself. And you are not making the mark on the world only you can make. Being loyal to your dreams is an essential building block to aging beautifully. Role models and mentors have their places, but only you have the power to embrace yourself just as you are.

Many of us grew up in families where our spiritual human development was thwarted. We learned that power existed in an outside authority and beliefs were set in stone. Under these circumstances it is hard to break the culturally driven, negative thoughts about aging so prevalent in society today.

Dearie, just do the best you can.

The following questions will organize your commitment to aging beautifully:

What calls you to take the journey of aging beautifully?
Why now?
Why is it you cannot afford to ignore this summons?

FOLLOW THE THREAD

The web is there for all of us; we are all weavers. Whatever a man does to the web, he does to himself.—Chief Seattle

I was seventy-two when I responded to an inner call to become a hospice volunteer.

I had planned on embracing hospice work when I retired. But at seventy-two there was no retirement in sight, so I decided not to postpone my wish any longer. I wanted to bring my gifts of attention and loving kindness to someone in their final stage of bare bones and stripping down. I remember my decision as a transforming moment. I called a hospice center and a strong voice on the other end said, "A training is about to begin. Please come in for an interview."

Our training occurred over several long weekends, and many fine hospice volunteers came to share their years of experience. None of them provided a profile of what constituted perfect hospice behavior. They talked about trusting their gut reactions and their desire to have an effect, whether large or small, on a person's dying experience. Eventually I came to discover that hospice work was a combination of compassion, presence, emotional stamina, and the courage to simply enter the room empty. One quickly got past the notion that a visit to a patient's bed was to be a particular way. It was best not to have a predetermined idea of what the hospice experience was or to dramatize it in any way. Visits were hard to measure, and I often had no indication that I was making a difference at all.

I have revisited my training many times over the years and remember with fondness the lessons our instructors imparted. There was a particularly poignant moment when our instructor introduced Anthony, a volunteer of fifteen years. She quickly gave him the floor, trusting his testimony to carry the nugget of his experience. He was a lovely, white-haired, soft-spoken man in his sixties, wearing a worn, brown leather jacket and soft trousers that do so much for a man's body. After briefly introducing himself, he said three words that found their way into the core of my being and continue to serve me to this day. His remark was both elegant and judicious. It eclipsed everything I had heard. He simply stated, "Follow the thread."

It was the best advice I could have gotten. Follow the thread invited me to come into the room empty every time. With that single directive, I was relieved of my own story and available to enter the patient's world. It was a place of empathic relationship where people do not have to speak in order to communicate. Wisdom, knowing, and intimacy owns the territory. By leaving judgment, rulebooks, and surface chatter behind, the room became a place of quiet source.

The thread was not found in the notion of how our time would be spent. My job was to be present and feel into the cues. That was the thread to follow. As I became more experienced, people's wishes, though subtle, became clear. Sometimes sitting by someone's bed was enough. Other times listening to me read from the Psalms was just too exhausting. Occasionally, the need was to speak about a family member with whom they were having difficulty. The thread was set by the patient and could be counted on to be a wise guide.

I learned over time that being a hospice volunteer was the observation of the nuanced experience of one person's final journey and the direct experience of being there for him or her.

Sitting with the dying is an extreme example of coming into the room empty. It is living in milliseconds without being encumbered by trying to get it right. You will always get it right when you are not bound by perfection.

The Wisdom Lesson

Every woman must ask herself if she is willing to tell the truth about what she really needs in order to protect her beauty.

A thread is a metaphor for the repetitive patterns of behavior that weave through our lives. They are the themes and plotlines that define us. How we think and what we do, over time, will create a thread. Identifying our aging thread is a powerful exercise in taking responsibility for our future.

We are each responsible for our aging thread. The task is to become conscious of our aging story and the way it influences our thinking. Accomplishing this task will serve you very well over the long haul.

Let's give birth to a new archetype of aging by designing an aging thread that brings astonishment and wonder into our lives. Let's refute the one-look-fits-all kind of beauty and live instead by the doctrine of beauty, presence, and detachment from the outcome as the model to follow.

I have led thousands of women's groups over the years, and the stories I heard still resonate within me. I recall a stocky, exhausted looking seventy-four-year-old woman wearing a black pantsuit and a crumpled, cotton blouse joining a newly formed Three Graces group. Most of the women were in their thirties and forties, and it was just wonderful to have an older woman in the room. After introducing herself, she looked me straight in the eye and said with anger and alarm, "No one has heard a thing I've said!" None of us moved. We all sat, stunned. As women, we understood exactly what she was saying. There are no age differences when a truth is being told. With that one sentence, she introduced a common thread to the room. We were women looking at our own stories and identified closely with hers. The stifling of women's voices has been a thread snaking through our lives for generations. She spoke for all of us.

Listening to another woman talk about her life triggers a cosmic recognition that facets of her experience are very like our own. It is a thread we share. It is not the particular woman in a story with whom we resonate as much as finding ourselves in empathetic relationship with her. We share the thread of not being taken seriously, not being heard. It has a familiar ring to it. When we listen to what is happening in the life of another, we are compelled to listen to the voices within ourselves because identification with others feeds the human desire to be known. Images haul up old memories, stir the fertile soil of feelings, make us rejoice in our resilience, and for many, someone else's story becomes the blessing that allow healing tears to flow.

A rich aging thread is an ally waiting to bless you each day. Trust the aging thread you have chosen, not the one society has chosen for you. Build a thread of self-respect and endless acts of kindness toward yourself.

A long time ago I wrote the following prayer. Let it bring solace to your process.

Wondering through the moonlight, I stopped.

Peering ahead with blind eyes, swallowing the thin, black air, and choking on the dark night pain,

I reached for a star. Then suddenly, the shroud lifted, and I was startled to find I had stumbled upon the beauty of my soul.

With these words of deep self-compassion, a woman can create a thread grounded in self-acceptance and grace. Imagine millions of women weaving threads that champion the cardinal rule. One thing is very clear: it is madness to allow commercial forces to decide what an aging thread should look like!

Allow this time of life to call you to new heights. Do not be deluded into thinking the journey of aging beautifully is self-serving or anything other than a spiritual path. We are traveling in the fields of surrender and respect for the whole.

- Was it ever necessary that you align yourself with your father against your mother?
- Were there different expectations of how your father aged verses how your mother aged?
- Is there a new aging family thread wanting definition?
- Finish the following sentence: "The aging thread running through my family was..."
- Revisit these sentences from time to time. Invite your family to join you.

SILENCE AND SOLITUDE

There is no cosmetic for beauty like happiness.—Countess of Blessington

Solitude is the experience of *choosing* to detach from the distractions and busyness of one's life to pursue instead the quiet of one's own company.

However solitude is expressed, for many, the day arrives when it is impossible to overlook the fact that solitude fills a need that people, money, or reputation cannot satisfy. Learning how to be alone, even for short periods of time, contributes to a beauty that leaves space for one's soul. Like a great symphony, solitude has the power to transport us beyond our small selves. It is worthy of every woman's consideration.

Many of us have been our own slave drivers. Solitude and rest were never given a moment's thought. For most of my life, solitude was only a concept, not at all essential and certainly not a serious way to live. It did not make much sense to me because there was so much work to be done! I thought solitude was for monks living on a mountain.

My life was a cornucopia of people with needs, demands, failings, and ambitions. Coming from a childhood home that was chronically unsafe and unpredictable, I was primed to develop a sixth sense and peripheral vision about people's needs. I was a born healer, so it was not surprising that I entered a profession centered on transition. I worked in the bountiful arena of the heart, and my entrepreneurial job description was a blank check to take care of everyone. I was in heaven.

My very real and honest love of people got perverted into an unhealthy attachment to making others happy. My innate gift of being able to respond to a need became subordinate to an inappropriate reaction to anyone who was hurting. Struggling with the real problems of others fed my addiction to making other people more important than my own health. There was no healthy choosing, only unhealthy reaction. Compulsion prohibited balance. I was blind to choice.

"You can't keep working like this. You will burn out," was the unsolicited advice a male colleague once gave me. I remember thinking how interesting it was for a man who usually kept his opinions to himself to go out on a limb and give me information he must have thought I needed. My terse reaction was, "Oh, no, I won't!" My quick response put an end to the subject before it had a chance to get off the ground. Nonetheless, his insightful comment registered. My justification for not taking care of my own needs was that I loved the kind of work I was doing, and I *was* doing the work I was born for; however, I did not understand that right livelihood does not preclude the need to withdraw from the world from time to time. I was flippant about the law of nature that says, "Everything needs to rest." Everything, that is, except me! The grandiosity of the addict was showing its colors, but I did not see it at all. Meanwhile, a gathering exhaustion was brewing.

The need to stop overworking, overachieving, and overfunctioning came about when I began to age and had to admit I was worn out. I could no longer pull myself together and soldier on as I had done a thousand times before. Body, mind, and soul I had reached my edge, and a week's rest or a month in Hawaii was not going to be enough to regain my stamina. I had dismissed something of the greatest import. I failed to heed the cardinal rule of protecting and nourishing my beauty. Somewhere in the love of my work, the people with whom I interacted, a healthy appetite for relationship, and just paying the bills, I failed to make critical decisions about my health and well-being. I did not listen to the warning signs my body was giving me. I was enchanted by the world and dangerously seduced into forgetting about myself. Under these conditions, I could not possibly go into the room empty!

A decision had to be made. I was either going to take care of myself or I was not. The demands of the world were never going to stop, and as I began to pull back and pull in, I swallowed my pride and admitted I was not superwoman. I had equated slowing down as failure. Admitting I was exhausted was actually freeing. I did not stop seeing friends or give up my professional obligations. But I did choose to give myself the solitude I needed from time to time.

As I arranged my life so that stretches of aloneness had a place in my appointment book, I began to fill up with a joy I had long forgotten. Selected solitude became a practice and impossible to live without. It was a grace requiring the grit of discipline and the love of breathing deeply again. I eased into it. And as I let go, I found my way back to my sweet, quieter nature.

But most important, solitude let me *feel*. I got in touch with the sadness of being on automatic pilot for so long. Moments of pure grief surfaced, allowing me to open to self-compassion. It felt wonderful! Easing up on heavy scheduling allowed me to calm down and breathe. And solitude led to empathy for other driven women. The more I surrendered, the more I seemed to have of myself. I met myself on the path of surrender, and I actually liked what I saw.

This change in behavior did not happen overnight. It took patience and saying no. It took letting go and the willingness to adapt to my own company.

Then something completely unexpected happened. I began to think of the aging process as my ally instead of my enemy. What an amazing bonus! Without the interference of outside voices, my inner life had the air to bubble up a new resolve of how I wanted to age.

No one could have convinced me that solitude was healing for body, mind, and spirit. I discovered that snippets of rest were not enough. What I needed was a commitment to the routine practice of telling the truth about what I needed.

Occasionally, when I am sitting alone in the dark, I feel the silence and it feels wonderful, and I never want to be without its rejuvenating spirit. There is where a spiritual root system feeds my heart and nurtures the love of my own company.

PART II

LET GO

To enter the transforming field of that much vaster vision is to learn how to be at home in change, and how to make impermanence our friend.

—Sogyal Rinpoche, from *The Tibetan Book of Living and Dying*

POCKETS

There is only one story. Every form of being is integral to this story. Nothing is itself without everything else having given shape and identity to everything else.—From *The Universe Story* by Brian Swimme and Thomas Berry

My mother always wanted me to buy her dresses that had two pockets. And I knew if I deviated from her instructions, there would rain down on me a tongue-lashing that could activate the fear and shame I had learned to keep under tight control. Her long years of confinement in a county institution destroyed all hope of her being able to embrace the invisible threads that bring families together in empathetic relationship. She was self-focused in the extreme. Whenever she struck out with vicious criticism, I easily came unglued and remained that way for days. The extreme confinement and repetition that characterized her life had molded her behavior into a volatile pattern of reaction to anyone who dared call her requests into question or had opinions other than her own.

At first, her demands felt unreasonable because it was difficult to find dresses with the type of pocket that met with her approval. At first her stringent requirements made little sense, but over time, I came to understand that two pockets sewn into the side seams of a dress contributed to her sense of place, a tiny, innocuous region she could call her own. They were little sanctuaries hidden away from the peering eyes of others. The pockets symbolized my mother's heart-wrenching attempts at establishing privacy in a world that offered none. She could hide her Camel cigarettes, cherry Life Savers, and collection of thick rubber bands inside them or slide her nicotine-stained fingers into the miniature chambers for a momentary feeling of comfort. The pockets were a grace announcing, "They have not stripped me of everything."

You see, Ellen Gertrude was *never* alone, *never* experienced silence, only occasionally encountered nature, and seldom observed variety in terms of people, food, or activities. My mother had few options and little choice. Living all day under the glare of fluorescent lights, the pockets were a reminder she had places into which no one could see, places she was not obligated to share. The pockets in Ellen Gertrude's dresses were her heroic attempt to retain a self, a completely nonviolent way of stating that her overseers did not direct all her actions. The pockets were a poignant reminder that in spite of her depressing circumstances she had a pitifully small but nonetheless real way of maintaining her own separateness while living for eighteen years in the confines of a county hospital for the mentally ill.

She lived in a starkly bare, heavily controlled hospital ward with forty women, all of whom were deeply troubled and heavily medicated. There was no place to set things down, no personal closet to store valuables, no special drawer to hold simple treasures. Chairs with plastic seats lined the sides of the four walls so the women sitting in them all day were forced to stare at one another from across the large room. High ceilings, linoleum floors, and a black-and-white TV were the backdrop for women who spent their days waiting for cigarette breaks, cajoling nurses for small favors, or simply staring into space. The place had a cursed, barren feel to it, as if someone had died there and no one informed the living that a dead woman was in the room. The overarching sense of disappointment carried a collective melancholy that got into the bones and stayed there. There was a lot of mourning to be done, but in this case, the living needed to mourn for themselves.

Specific days were scheduled when the patients walked in lines down long halls to a large, tiled room where they showered together. Eyes lowered and backs turned in a feeble attempt to hide their naked bodies from one another. Like small children who believe that if they covered their faces no one will see them, forty women did their best to mask feelings of public embarrassment. Toilet stalls with no doors completed the indignity. They were all lumped together as if they had never been somebody before they came to Hawthorne Hospital for the Mentally Ill, as if they had never been sweet, dewy girls busy with dreams and plans for womanhood, as if they had never rocked babies to sleep or comforted worn-out husbands with the solace of a thousand kisses. It was hard to imagine they had ever been young. Their segregation from society was complete, and it showed in the imposed restriction of originality. These outcasts were all lumped together. Silence and solitude, spiritual qualities so necessary for embracing good health, were not to be found in the ward called Unpredictable. Instead, the confluence of sameness and imbalance had its way in this colorless place. The patients all had complicated problems, but the foul air they breathed came close to guaranteeing that self-respect would wither and souls would get sucked dry.

Gradually my mother lost track of how long she had been in the hospital. She forgot why she was in the hospital. She forgot that the sheer number and potency of her epileptic seizures had irrevocably altered her sweet and loving nature. There were periods when she grudgingly accepted her circumstances and other times when she raged and raged and raged. The reality was that she was institutionalized at the age of forty-seven after eighteen years of battling seizures and the severe personality distortion that changed her. Year after year, the violence rising from thousands of seizures gathered its pain, throwing my father, brother, and me around like rag dolls. It formed us in profound ways. My brother and I developed a high degree of compassion and human understanding for the neglected and suffering of the world. At the same time I was learning that the needs of others came first. There was no healthy choosing, just unhealthy reacting.

But nobody suffered as she did. The day the door to freedom clanged shut behind her, Ellen Gertrude said good-bye to hundreds of freedoms, both great and small: when to eat, what to eat, when to sleep, what time to turn the lights out, when to wash her hair, who to spend time with, if she could have a visitor, what to do with the visitor, how long the visitor could stay, when to use the telephone, and when, if ever, she could open the big glass door to the outside world and shut it behind her for good.

Stripping someone spiritually, psychologically, and emotionally makes that person very vulnerable to the system that disrobed them. They become depersonalized, wounded sparrows, rendered helpless and left to the mercy of their captors. Eventually the life force is reduced to a flicker, and what is left is a lump of clay. And clay was what the women became—malleable, dry, and old. The group identity that was stamped on the psyche of each was that they were not individuals, nor were they anyone special. In these circumstances, people become obsessed with the smallest things, and two pockets sewn into a dress take on an amplified meaning. The value of the pockets was blown all out of proportion. Yet, it was Ellen Gertrude's attempt to cleave to something, no matter how seemingly insignificant, that contributed to the sense of being somebody.

All forty women, including my mother, lived out their entire lives in these circumstances. Throughout the eighteen years I visited her, I sensed her weariness. It was a weariness born of a system overcrowded, underfunded, and unable to respond to the basic need for self-respect and personal pride. Gradually my mother lost track of how long she had been in the hospital. She forgot why she was in the hospital in the first place. She forgot that the magnitude of her epileptic seizures had bred a personality distortion that altered her very nature. There were times when she grudgingly accepted her circumstances and other times when she raged and raged and raged. The sad reality was that her wings had been clipped once she entered the cage of sameness and perpetual control. Ultimately, each woman was on her own to navigate the labyrinth of nurses, doctors, grimy cafeterias, and ancient red-brick buildings with bars on dirty windows. The Unpredictables, as they were called, all had complicated emotional problems, but the air they breathed came close to guaranteeing their self-worth would wither. Exposure to my mother and the thirty-nine women she lived with raised my level of awareness to the plight of the disinherited, disengaged, and discouraged. Superficiality never gained a foothold in my own psyche, but if it did, a visit with my mother brought me back to the sobering reality that for a segment of society, shapeless days and stone-dead nights are standard. This lesson equated to more than the adage, "Count your blessings." I was witnessing coping skills at the highest level. Whenever I observed the thirty-nine women Ellen Gertrude lived with, all with their identical bowl-shaped haircuts, cotton housedresses, pasty-looking skin, and nicotine-stained fingers, it became clear that monotony, struggle, and suffering are tragically the rule of the day for many. It was a heartbreaking scene that amplified small surges of diversity and made them all the more precious.

My worst nightmare was that my father would die before my mother. That nightmare came to pass when my father died two years before her. My brother and I dutifully continued my father's ritual of providing her new paperback novels, cherry Life Savers, roast beef sandwiches on soft white bread, and Camels. In truth, I did not always look forward to visiting my mother and was usually spurred on by obligation. No matter how many times the scene was reenacted, how many times I settled my fractured nerves, gave myself a pep talk, or received sympathy from outsiders, a visit with my mother was always the same. I was on edge, waiting for a seizure and the catastrophe that invariably followed. I never found a way around that feeling. I operated from a routine of doing what was expected of me and tried hard to put my feelings aside. Adolescent years of feeling unsafe and vulnerable around her settled deep inside me, and I became an acutely observant and discerning adult with reservoirs of courage for the moments when I needed to fight for my life.

The women living in the confines of the hospital were hard-pressed to manipulate outer forces, and each had to decide what small measures would make life tolerable. I doubt very much my mother was conscious of the impact her everyday realities were having on me. Without a doubt, she was a teacher showing me life in a raw form. But she alone made the convoluted journey through a maze of pills, psychiatrists, lousy food, stagnant air, too much sugar, and too many cigarettes.

She lived as one of society's marginalized but found infinitesimal ways to push the edge. She taught me invaluable lessons about the freedom to choose and enjoyment of little things. My mother spun gold by making simple things blindingly vivid, and I have benefited every day of my life from those lessons.

But I have early childhood memories. I recall young mothers sitting on the stoop on steamy New Jersey summer nights. They sat with bare legs, gossiping and smoking Camel cigarettes while watching their children play kick-the-can in the street. Husbands were off downing cool beers at Harry's Bar where they recuperated from another day at their despised make-do jobs where they knew they were painted into a corner. But there was rent to be paid and kids to feed. Theirs was a tradeoff between the bosses who exploited them and the sweet women they returned to each night.

It was an unspoken rule that the women of Prospect Avenue only ventured out to Harry's Bar on Saturday night. That's when they dolled up. They blatantly used their sexuality in a premeditated plot to arouse the desire of their hard-working men. They painted lips that were still full a dark red and put on tight-fitting crepe dresses that exploited their asses. An undercurrent of sexuality permeated the damp, smoke-filled air of Harry's. Someone banged away at the out-of-tune piano, and women took turns sitting on top of it, lifting their dresses to expose some thigh while pretending to be Rita Hayworth. Their goddess wares were on display, and they quite loved it.

Everyone tried to take in as much as possible. They drank, smoked, cursed, laughed, complained, gossiped, and raged against Washington. Call Harrys a relief or an escape, the saloon lifted the flatness and routine from their lives. And when Harry's shut it's doors at 2:00 a.m. and they lumbered home in committed twos, the women's hot bodies eagerly yielded to husbands who had been stirred up all night by sensuous laughter and swaying hips.

Conditions were raw there, and it would be easy to judge the Prospect crowd as crude. But conditions brought out a shrewdness often seen in people who live on the edge. The lack of money tested their mettle day after day, and in the process, they became very resourceful about getting their needs met.

Filling up on a Saturday night kept their insides from being sucked out by the system that kept them in place. The women in particular demonstrated a cultural shrewdness that mothers raising children on bare bones are forced to develop. They were all the same, these women who sat on the stoop. And my mother was one of them. They shared a youthful, sassy vigor, a code of silence about what went on behind the closed doors of their simple rooms where there was not enough furniture to make the place look nice, never enough heat coming from the coal furnace in winter, or good screening to keep the mosquitoes out in the summer. Of course, there was never enough money. However, they developed acute coping skills born of the consistent, emotionally exhausting task of making ends meet. It was a fragile, no-frills, meta-edge society. Dining rooms and extra towels were not to be found anywhere.

But no doubt, the Prospect community had a sense of place to it. The young families shared working-class values that fostered bonds of intimacy.

The Prospect Avenue women and the Unpredictable women were each a small but distinct universe requiring every drop of survivalist ingenuity a person could conjure up. Both societies were vulnerable to an outer-directed authority, and each woman had to make a choice as to how she would make life work for her. Though barely discernible to an unpracticed eye, the women were heroic figures demonstrating that no matter how compromised, life was not set in stone. There was room for a voice, however small. Every choice was a cosmic grace of its own. Each society was its own matrix out of which something else originated.

My mother was almost sixty-five the last time I saw her in May 1975. In someone's care, she was allowed to leave the hospital grounds for four hours. It was always the event of the week for her. I had taken her for a drive and made the ritual presentation of roast beef sandwiches on soft white bread, cherry Life Savers, strong coffee laced heavily with sugar, paperback novels, and Camel cigarettes. She looked very gray that spring day, and when at five o'clock we said good-by outside the ward, she stood looking up at me for what seemed a very long time. I bent down, kissed her good-bye, and drove the one and a half hours to my home at the Jersey Shore. As I pulled into the driveway of my little blue house with its sparkling clean, white café curtains hanging in eight big, clean windows, I could see my husband and five children seated around the maple dining room table waiting for me. I was glad to be home, felt my body relax, and quickly put the day behind me.

The next morning I received a 6:00 a.m. call from the hospital. The male voice on the other end said, "I regret to inform you that your mother died peacefully in her sleep at four thirty this morning."

It was a few days before her sixty-fifth birthday, and in the eighteen years of living at Hawthorne Hospital, she had dwindled to a fraction of the sweet, good-hearted woman I barely remember but had heard about all my life. Blessedly, the end came quickly. There would be no more suffering. She had suffered enough. It was over. Surrounded by thirty-nine women, all lying in their metal beds, my mother let go and went to her heavenly home.

My husband and I had been planning a family trip to Yellowstone National Park for over a year and decided to take her with us. We searched carefully for a good spot in which to lay her cremains. As my children looked on, I buried her ashes and crushed bones in the soft earth surrounding a tall pine tree. I knew she would love coming to this final resting place because Ellen Gertrude had never been west of the Mississippi, and Yellowstone carried the breath of life while asking nothing of her in return. It was a spirited piece of earth, perfect for a woman who had been restrained by illness nearly her entire adult life. The demon had extracted so much. Now she was free. There would be no more falling, swallowing lit cigarettes, or feeling the agonizing pain of a burnt mouth. She lay perfect in the arms of God now.

I am so proud of my mother. To this day I never look at pockets without thinking of the grace she unknowingly wove into my life.

There was a time if you told me I would someday be thanking my mother for teaching me about deep seeing and compassion, I would have thought you were crazy. But time and experience has a way of taking us to inner places we need to go.

When I put her story on the page, she became a person I could look at without being overwhelmed. I met her where she was and saw a frightened, deeply hurt woman fighting everyday for her life. It gave me the focus to go beyond ordinary sight and into the underbelly of her real existence. I gave her the dignity she deserved and compassion bubbled up. Her essence is an important part of my own journey, and I will forever take her with me.

Wisdom Lesson

Making your mother a real person with human flaws will help you in your quest to age beautifully. By making peace with your mother and how she has influenced you, all manner of truths will become clear. Let go. Give peacemaking the heart it needs.

You will be beautifully served by understanding your mother.

Knowing who she was, the life stages that most impacted her, the dreams she failed to fulfill, her relationship with marriage, the events that changed her life, and the fears surrounding her own aging process are considerations that all lead back to you. Discovering what your mother's life was about, not just as a mother but as a woman, is a wisdom search that will serve you well over time. Understanding the most influential woman in your life is a task that *cannot* be dismissed. In forty years of working with women, healing the mother/daughter relationship ranks high on the list of issues still screaming for resolution.

The purpose of understanding your mother is not to shame her, judge her, prosecute her, or change her. Make your mother a real person, and you will be led to the sacred field of separation from her. You will be freed to pursue the things that make aging beautifully possible.

Whether you are estranged from your mother or adore the ground she walks on, it is important to know what makes her tick. It is not essential that you agree with her, like her, love her, or even want to be in her company. What *is* essential is that you understand her. You did not walk in her shoes, but you inhabited her belly. Nothing alters the fact that long ago the two of you began a journey together. Nothing can change that.

Maybe your mother is difficult or maybe she is your best friend. Perhaps she doesn't listen, doesn't like your husband, your haircut, your taste in clothes, your eating habits, your career choice, thinks you are wasting money on yoga classes, is certain you spend too much money traveling to Paris, is certain your health insurance is bogus, and wishes you would get a real job instead of being a painter. Maybe the relationship has, in fact, little going for it. You might not like her or have ever had a meaningful communication with her. You might not feel love for your mother. Perhaps you never met your biological mother and do not want to meet her. Perhaps you were raised by a warm-hearted adoptive mother who loved and nurtured you from the beginning. She might be the woman who is tied to your heartbeat. The point is you will understand yourself better when you understand your mother and the story you have about her.

Gathering information about your mother will not work the same for everyone. Go easy. You might get nowhere or you might be surprised. It is best not to have expectations. If you find she is resistant to letting you in, you must make peace with that fact. Even her deathbed might not be enough to soften the edges that had long ago turned to stone. Go gently, sing yourself a lullaby. It is not easy having a rejecting mother.

The experience of being raised by a mentally ill mother is not most people's experience, but it was mine. After looking at the pain and shame I have carried, I have come to realize who my mother really was, and I have forgiven her for the terrifying nights and confusing days that filled my early years. All her rage and jealousy, destructive behavior and violent outbursts, the embarrassing behaviors that kept friends and family gossiping about us—everything has been forgiven. And I have forgiven myself for using control and worldly success as methods for feeling safe.

In the process of understanding her, I have fallen in love with her. My investigation has had shaping power over my life, and I am proud to say she is in me. Had I not observed firsthand what it was like to be denied freedom of movement or even the possibility of integration into the larger culture, I would have missed a deeply humanizing lesson.

Looking into my mother's life was the gateway to examining meaning in other areas of my life. I found meaning in the professional work I was so well-suited for, in the computer screen that served my writer's heart, and in the testimony of hundreds of brave women who were on their own road to healing. Meaning found me in the lives of my children, in prayer, and in the arms of safe men. It does not matter that it has taken until my seventies to begin rooting this out. The creases on my face are softer now, heroism is more treasured, and I think of my mother as a champion. The bonding that occurred at the start of our journey and got so badly short-circuited has come back with an intimate feel.

Her name was Ellen Gertrude McMahon, and she was my mother.

Wisdom Lesson

The following are suggestions that may help you come to peace with your mother.

Sit with her and ease into the suggestion that she write a short heirloom piece. The purpose is (1) to let her have her say; (2) to leave her heirs her own response to her own life; and (3) to let go.

You might give her prompts, such as: "All my life..." or "When I was young, I thought..." or "I once believed...but now I see..."

This is not about perfect sentences, spelling, or grammar. This is about letting your mother have her voice without correction or criticism from you. Mothers are notoriously defensive. I have met very few mothers who wouldn't like to go back and do some things differently. Keep in mind she is a female human being first and your mother second.

Your first goal is to help her feel safe. If she wants to talk, wonderful. If she can only communicate in terse statements for five minutes, that is what it will have to be. You can pick up the conversation at another time. What is of utmost importance is that she does not get the impression you are out to make her wrong! Many mothers have been deeply hurt even if they do not know it. Caution is advised. This assignment can be accomplished over time. Explore her life process as if taking a feather to a fine piece of Chippendale furniture.

Have respect for your courage in taking this task on. Sing yourself another lullaby.

FORGIVENESS HELPED ME TO LET GO

There is no future without forgiveness.—Archbishop Desmond Tutu

For many years I met regularly with a group of female friends, all in their forties. They were beautiful, sassy, smart, intuitive, hard-working women with hearts of gold. There was Debra, the fab international makeup consultant; Judy, the spectacular red-headed matchmaker; and Rosanne, the brilliant corporate consultant. We were prayer partners when we spoke on the telephone, but when we gathered monthly, we called our meetings "Men, Magic, and Manifesting." And oh, what marvelous evenings they became. It was a monthly ritual: a shared bottle of champagne, a big, healthy salad, a ravishing dessert, and hours of talk about finding good men and manifesting the kind of career wealth where we made a difference in the world. We had stories to tell and never tired of giggling our way through the telling. But as the evening wore on and we were buzzed a little, our conversations took on the feel of a labyrinth talk. We circled around until we found ourselves reflecting on the blessing of the spiritual path. Our hearts swelled and the room grew warm with thoughts of faith. It was easy to feel blessed and young in spirit.

Our one-on-one telephone conversations were more focused. I spoke to Rosanne often, and before we hung up she told me what she wanted me to pray for for her, and I told her what I wanted her to pray for, for me. Then we hung up. Sitting in the comfort of our apartments, from across the city in San Francisco, we prayed for each other. It was a practice we both loved.

Over years of conversation, we covered every conceivable subject, learning a great deal about each other in the process. In the middle of a discussion on forgiveness, Rosanne simply asked, "Have you forgiven your ex-husband?" I mumbled a no answer and changed the subject. But the topic was on the table. "Of course I have forgiven him!" I said before hanging up. That lasted for a total of forty-eight hours, and I was back to square one. The truth was I had not forgiven him. I had my long list of grievances and justifications for not forgiving. I was heavily invested in defending and blaming so as to maintain the superiority of being right. Of course, this misguided mechanism destroyed any possibility of approaching the well of forgiveness and distanced me from the genuine expression of grief that could have been the outlet for letting go. I was not willing to see him as a man of his generation, nor was I willing to understand the wounds that he, like all of us, carry. I cut him no slack whatsoever.

There I was, twenty years after our divorce, still holding vengeance in my heart. The day had come for me to consider some serious acts of generosity and forgiveness. I was committed to a spiritual life and determined to shine a light on forgiveness as the heroic act that could heal of us both.

I thought about it every day. I was not obsessed, but if twenty years after our divorce I was still resentful of a man with whom I had shared a bed, built a genuine life, and brought five children into world, then I had not learned much about the spiritual path. I was not letting go, I was hanging on. If I wanted meaning, compassion, and texture in my life, I best be walking the talk. This process was not going to be about meditations, mantras, and prayer partners anymore. It was time to see the man's inner beauty and human flaws as a person walking the earth doing the best he could. I did not choose an action for accomplishing forgiveness. Rosanne and I did not even go back to the forgiveness talk. I went about my business, but something unnamable followed me. In a strange way, forgiveness walked with me. I had decided to understand him, be more sensitive to his own fragile beginnings, to his fear of change, intense negativity, and mistrust of people, and yes, to his decency, steadiness, wonderful work ethic, and love of nature. My intention was to forgive my ex-husband of twenty-seven years. Several months later, when I was not thinking about anything in particular, it came in an instant, "Yes, Jim, I forgive you." There were no flashes of light, no bells and whistles. It was sudden, unceremonious but profoundly real. I chose a path of grace and heightened compassion for the misfortunes of his life and the bitterness that lived in his ancestry. Several months later, I felt a deep down, overwhelming flood of love for a man I had never once in twenty-seven years of marriage felt for him. In my quest to forgive, I befriended myself and unearthed a voice that was willing to do the authentic work of letting go.

Shortly thereafter, I heard he was very ill. We had not spoken in years. I called and though our conversation was brief, it held the seeds of restoration for us both. He and I had made a long journey together and forgiveness put closure on it for me. It is good to live with that. My friend had placed the table before me, and I followed the thread to a beautiful conclusion. I had forgiven. It was no longer a truce. It was a surrender. Forgiving Jim was a choice that set me free. When I made the intention to forgive, I felt I was going into an eerily dark forest without a compass. Forgiving *is* unknown territory. It *is* a journey we take alone regardless of how many books we read, gurus we follow, or wonderful conferences and workshops we attend. I was afraid that by forgiving him, I would have to deny the legitimate loneliness that characterized much of the marriage from the beginning. For a long time I nurtured my resentment and clung to having been wronged. But that kept me in chains. It took a long time but forgiveness healed the bitter resentment I carried from having given my youth to a man so ill-suited to me.

With the passage of time, forgiveness emptied me, leaving me room to appreciate the simple, everydayness of the marriage. Regret, resentment, and reproach are no longer what I feel when I think of him. I put down the gauntlet of indictment, let go of the corrosive nature of blame, and finally gave the man his due. What was left were feelings of relatedness, compassion, and the knowledge that he and I wove thousands of powerful family threads together. Many of these threads were valuable and worthy of being woven into the fabric of the next generation. Others were discarded because they carried the joyless seeds of revenge. When I openly worried that my prolonged unforgiveness might have hurt my children, a beloved daughter said, "Mom, we are all smart and beautiful, and we all work hard. Mom, we have good bones. Don't worry so much!"

Was the marriage perfect? Far from it. But it happened, and I have put it in its proper place. I can let it be over. I accept him. And perhaps, most important of all, I no longer carry negative vibes into conversation with my children in regard to their father. I tell the truth, but it is not laced with being right. I began talking about the good times. Our first funky apartment, his tenacity about steam cleaning the motor of his cars and painting the sparkplugs gold, his willingness to spend four hours in our very cramped attic on Christmas Eve putting doll houses and bicycles together, and his major feeling of accomplishment when he drove all seven of us from New Jersey to Florida in nineteen hours, stopping only for gas and very, very quick trips to gas station bathrooms.

Without a doubt, forgiveness was an act of justice that balanced my life and brought me back to praise.

Wisdom Lesson

Forgiveness is the greatest beauty compound of them all.

You might be asking, "What does forgiveness have to do with aging beautifully?" The answer is everything. Peace of mind is written on the face. It gives a woman a special brand of beauty that no surgeon's knife can achieve. Mark my words, there will be no beautiful aging without forgiveness being present in your life.

Nothing is more raw than the act of forgiving. Nothing comes from a deeper well nor gives more meaning to the term *spiritual practice* than does the act of forgiving. Just the intention to forgive will bring you before your own mirror to face a rich and deepened self.

Forgiveness is radical. It is powerful and can change a woman. It is serious business that touches the bone and brings grief to front stage. Forgiveness is a combination of letting go of the victim role, giving up our determination to be right, and gathering the courage to make the clear decision to get on with life. It is not easy to look at the hurting parts of ourselves, but if we are to forgive another, the assignment is to do just that. Forgiveness has to do with summoning the courage to break free of punishing memories, haunting regrets, poor choices, and the sting of self-betrayal. By making the decision to forgive yourself and/or others, you will be embracing two strong, human potentialities: our deep capacity to surrender and our enormous potential to change.

One way to heal is to reach out to a few safe people and ask them to listen to your story one last time. Tell them this will be the last drip, drip,

drip of accusation and complaints. It is the last litany of grief keeping your open wound alive. Tell your story with a performance worthy of an Academy Award. Ask these trusted souls to hold you and listen to you as you express how hard it is to give up your stuff, how much your memories keep you awake at night. Tell them you want to forgive. Ask for their opinion, their praise, their love, and their help. Ask for lullabies. Tell them you are willing to let go. Tell them you want to age beautifully, but unforgiveness keeps a frown on your forehead and locks in a dampened smile. Tell them you are tired of unfinished business holding you back. Tell them.

Forgiveness is a freedom passage. Nothing replaces meeting with one's own subterranean realm, the place where the shadow lives and projections are used to limp along with a half-life, where things are "fine" but not felt, where distraction is deadening and the tree never comes to leaf. Explanations of compassion can fall short. Add forgiveness and one can easily get in trouble. It is simply best to tell what happened and feel the hurt, the bitter pill, and the shipwreck of being lied to, stolen from, betrayed, and left for dead. Tell the truth, but *feel* the injury. You are with friends who are not going to let you down. The strength and sweet notes of your soul are not going to let you down. Trust the mystery. The time of waiting for things to take care of themselves is over.

Do this and you will never again hide from your greatness. You will become everything the cardinal rule is about.

Here then is the task: (1) you must forgive others for the crimes, both great and small, that have been perpetuated against you. Until you have the intention to begin doing this, you will continue to foster the curse of ill will, vindictiveness, and victimhood. The resentment you harbor will be your downfall, both body and soul; (2) you must forgive yourself for the ways in which you perceive you have hurt yourself and others. The freedom of self-love and personal redemption will elude you until you start accepting your own heartfelt sorrow for mistakes, oversights, errors in judgment, and careless thinking.

> Set the light low. Breathe. Let your mind go.
>
> * Write down what you are feeling at this moment.
> * What people immediately come to mind? Does this topic upset you?
> * Are you willing to address this task head-on?
> * Think of someone you have been unwilling to forgive.
> * Write down his or her name, the issue, and your intention.
> * Write down why it has taken you so long to forgive.
> * Write down how much you have enjoyed holding on.
> * Write the truth.

Buy yourself a small forgiving bowl. It can be a precious heirloom or something you buy at the Dollar Store. Place it where you will see it each day. On your night table, kitchen cabinet, bathroom sink, your desk, or any surface that will catch your eye. Fill it with water, add a few rose petals, colorful marbles, or whatever strikes your fancy. As you glance at the bowl each day, state your intention to forgive.

In your mind's eye, see all tightness around your mouth, eyes, and forehead dissolve. The next time you spot your forgiving bowl, gently repeat your intention to forgive. State your intention in positive terms, such as, "I am forgiving..."

* Feel your way along, and remember that something creative is happening.

Forgiving is the masterpiece of your spiritual work in this lifetime. Nothing you do will be more important, more esteem building or more ennobling than forgiving that which caused you pain. Bring out your grief. It is the road to freedom. Stop trying to look good because we usually do not look good when we are experiencing pain. Self-compassion is crucial here. You are building your core. Trust forgiveness. Trust your feelings. The day has arrived when blocking out sorrow, anger, and disappointment is no longer an option.

This is a day for celebration. Nothing develops more peace of mind, wisdom, and inner beauty than knowing you are willing to change.

Dear God,
    Pieces fall off me.
    I am turning into dust.
    Soon the pain will be gone,
    only a pile of dried-up despair will lie on my bed.
    God,
    stay with me
    as I come back to life.

THE OLDER WOMAN AND HER YOUNG MAN

To thine own self be true.—William Shakespeare

Any woman who has a love affair with a man who is the same age as her adult children will never be the same again.

I knew this in the depth of my being as I began my love affair with Scott. He at twenty-five and I at fifty made quite a couple! We differed in age, lifestyle, vocation, income, friends, work habits, dress, philosophy, religion, politics, and experience. Where we met was in the mystery of the heart.

Something in me was profoundly moved when I met Scott. I cannot say what it was exactly, only that when I fell in love with him I touched an unexplored and raw side of my womanhood. I felt joy and revelation on a level I had only experienced in the delivery room. It was more than the high new lovers know. It was more like the shock of discovering some nebulous something inside me, a thing that seemed dead for lack of psychic air, was now deeply alive.

Was I resonating with a primordial life force that had lain dormant until now? Had I innocently stumbled into a wakefulness so powerful my body came alive in ways that felt new yet remarkably ancient? Whatever it was, my ripe feminine presence had found the warmth of the sun. I was being discovered and recognized moment by moment, kiss by kiss.

Scott was strangely free of attachments and seemed so stunningly pure to me. All six feet, four inches of him radiated an unpretentious man who was comfortably free of society's attempts to force him into a particular mold. His slender body showed itself under tight jeans and his jet-black beard framed pink lips whose fullness seemed to want touch. His large hands fascinated me. I was captivated by his simple gesture of swirling a tea bag in a mug of hot water. Even the way he carefully turned down the bedcovers at day's end was special. Everything seemed tender and important. I had never seen this level of sensitivity in a man.

He was a sound engineer with a local rock band and worked late into the night, often arriving at my bed at three in the morning after the Asbury Park clubs closed. I always left the front door unlocked so he could tiptoe up the white-carpeted stairs to my second-floor bedroom. I lay in my high four-poster bed pretending to be asleep, but I was always awake and wild with anticipation. There, kneeling beside my bed for what felt like a long time, he spoke my name, "Ilene, Ilene." Then his hands found me under the ice-blue satin sheets. He touched me fiercely and gently, invoking a magic that took my breath away. He was a black-haired angel who appeared at the right time in the collapsing, stress-filled world of divorce.

Scott taught me that sex was a by-product of deep intimacy. It was sacredness birthing a holy night and required the art of surrender. We sang sweet lullabies to the world and leaned into the taproot of expectancy. We lay for hours in the sweat of our own thirsty loins and kissed until our lips were numb. We thought we felt the earth shudder and mountains push heavenward. After twenty-seven years of marriage I was discovering what it was like to hear my name spoken as if it mattered. At age forty-eight, I was learning how to be close to a man.

We met in philosophy class where we indulged in self-analysis and read *Man's Search for Himself* by Rollo May. Our friendship was only cursory, so I was surprised to receive a call from him several years after we graduated. "I've just read the *Women's Room*," he said. "I'm fascinated and thought you would be the perfect person to give me a feminist perspective. Would you care to go to lunch?"

We met at a local café, the kind with red Formica tabletops and wonderful, friendly waitresses. But there was little discussion of the book. Sitting across from one another, there was an unspoken energy that wanted expression. Seated in the crowded café, we could not have known the road we were embarking upon. I invited him to accompany me to a place of beauty I knew best, a spot where God's hand was clearly visible. "Would you care to go to the beach tomorrow night?" I asked.

The next night we found ourselves walking the boardwalk that paralleled the beautiful Jersey coastline. We walked in silence for a long time before we stopped to face each other. The moonlight outlined our bodies and stoked our passion. We kissed. Surprised by our assertiveness, Scott stepped back, a questioning expression on his handsome face. "It's okay," I said. "Really, it's okay for us to feel this." He tossed his gorgeous head backward and laughed from deep within himself. "I'd forgotten how marvelous it is to be alive and feel the joy of a spontaneous moment," he cried.

And so began a three-year love affair that altered my life forever. We became two souls that loved each other from the core of our beings. Two minds that learned how to let go of society's rules and make time stand still. Two bodies that discovered the awe and satisfaction found in the rarefied air of lust. As if I were a virgin seeking her first entry, I let him devour me, fill me up on honey. I had been held in the grip of an empty cup for so long that drinking him in brought the sound of soft wind blowing through my loins.

I often thought lovers swallowed each other. Could I swallow youth? Swallow youth! What a thought! Yes, taking him in brought young energy to my flesh, and I shed psychological years like a snake sheds its skin. I was wet, fertile, innocent, and famished, and despite our age difference, just as pure as he was. Decades of unmet emotional needs were suddenly meeting the thirsty undiscovered self that had been exiled years before. The romantic canvas on which I was painting new dreams was literally in my hands, and a new me was discovering my goddess nature.

It was very clear that Scott was not Prince Charming coming to solve my problems and carry me into the sunset. He was a gifted young man who could talk and listen and then sit naked on the end of my bed and sing to me. At such moments, his beautiful voice carried out past the blue, sheer, curtained windows. These were the hot, humid, summer nights that gave neighbors something to gossip about! But he was bringing innocence and naiveté to the little girl inside that had been forgotten. I was being appreciated. I glowed. I took it all in. His love was like balm on a wound I was not conscious of having. We stopped comparing ourselves with other couples and enjoyed the freedom of determining our own lives. It was a risk to get out of the box society wanted to put us in. It meant reevaluating our relationship over and over, giving up control of what we knew to move into a life without chronological boundaries. The result was a period of unparalleled creativity in many areas of my life, and my children seemed more precious than ever because I respected their rights as I began to value my own.

I was concerned about the effect my relationship would have on my children. My oldest daughter was older than my lover! My teenage sons were understandably confused at first, but they loved having a man around who played the guitar, wrote music, and sang like an angel. They loved the sincere interest he took in them. Scott respected them and it showed. Our first Christmas together found the family gathered in the evening, eagerly giving Scott the stage to serenade us. We were dreamy and full. We were comfortable and content and enthralled. Great gifts were bestowed on my children that Christmas night. They learned their mother was a person, a sexual being capable of romance and seeking it in a different way. And they learned that they too could grow in new and wondrous ways at any age.

Celebrating my fiftieth birthday lives on in a class by itself. Art, rapture, joy, love, gratitude, surprise, luxury, sex, splendor—the night had it all, and I have revisited that birthday night many times over the years. Unknown to me Scott had found a book of large lithographs in a ramshackle antique shop. The book was filled with black and white images of women ranging in age from infancy to death. Some were fourteen by seventeen, others were twenty-three by seventeen. He selected thirteen of the most stunning, named and numbered them, put them in sequence, had them matted, and wrapped each in violet flowered paper. They portrayed: infancy, girlhood, adolescence, womanhood, and points of female development that he gave name to: trust, lover, motherhood, emerging self, friendship, teacher, triumph of angels, and death. These lithographs became my most prized possession from the very start. Currently they hang on a beautiful gray wall in my living room. I regularly use them in my work with women and writers groups. And I love them as much today as the July night I received them. The lithos continue to speak to me, as they do to other women, helping them to recognize parts of themselves they might have disowned but need to reclaim. The lithographs capture the journey.

What I remember most about my fiftieth birthday was that I felt seen. He knew me. He said, "Ilene, these lithographs are you." It was glorious and so unfamiliar that I swooned until I thought I would pass out. After each opening we made love or went to the beach, bought chocolate ice-cream cones, we laughed, we cried, and could not get enough of each other.

Part of the ceremony of giving was that I opened them one at a time and in sequence. It took hours. There has never been another night like it.

In spite of all the lust, juice, and jazz, it was not enough to hold our relationship together, and after three years we began to slowly come apart. Our different value systems separated us, the disparity in our work ethic, life goals, and the wide breach of developmental stages became too different to ignore and impossible to traverse. But to this day we talk about what took place in that magical space we once occupied. We were mentor and teacher to one another. We were the best of friends. We were a support system, a network of two communing with bravado over the twenty-three years that separated us. We loved our age difference and never tired of talking about it, believing that our age difference was also our ally. We proved to ourselves for all time that body and soul, we were the same.

I loved him deeply. I shall always love him deeply. How could I ever feel old? There is no age in the very heart of things, and my experience has shown me that agelessness is real and attainable. I love knowing this truth and experience a freeing grace in my life. I have my memories. With the passage of time, they still taste sweet on my lips.

Wisdom Lesson

The combination of having brains, discernment, and human understanding *plus* being desirable, delicious, and experienced in bed certainly qualifies you for having your act together. Start calling yourself a feminist goddess. You have earned it!

The tale told here is not an invitation to start dating younger men. It is a story illustrative of thinking outside the box, challenging the status quo, daring to be different, loving your body no matter how old it is and what shape it's in, risking gossip, jeopardizing family acceptance, gambling on approval, and chancing being laughed at, which all fall into the messy category of societal pressure. Aging beautifully has a great deal to do with looking back on our lives and feeling a sense of completeness. No regrets.

I would like to pass along the secret to finding love, allure, and sexual potency with a younger man. *Believe you are beautiful, valuable, and desirable. Believe that a young man is fortunate to have your very good company. Everyone deserves love. Let go of what others think.*

> * If you are considering dating a much younger man, these are questions I suggest you ask yourself
> * Am I safe here?
> * What am I hoping for?
> * Do I sincerely care about what I bring to him?
> * What is the most difficult part about dating a younger man?
> * Am I prepared for the time when he will leave me?
> * Am I being honest? Will I let go with grace?
> * Is the relationship an ego trip, therefore carrying with it an unhealthy agenda?

LIFE WAS EASIER WHEN THEY WERE SMALL

Let no one be deluded that knowledge of the path can substitute for putting one foot in front of the other.—M. C. Richards

When I turned seventy-five my children gave me a birthday party.

Their acknowledgement of me as the mother who had showed them how to care for life took my breath away. By the end of day four, I felt as if redemption had planted its rainbow at my feet, and for the rest of my days I would walk the earth with peace. The experience was far more than five adult children demonstrating their love and appreciation to the mother who raised them. It was a celebration of life.

I had nothing to do with the preparations and knew little of the events that were planned. The cascade of tears, the level of awe, the testimonies, the generosity, the reminiscing, the cooperation, the surprises, and the willingness to have the rawest of feelings exposed held me captive, thrilling me, and bringing me to a state of near emotional collapse. I have pictures, a video, pages of written testimony, and marvelous images burned into my memory.

I want that birthday weekend to replicate itself. I want everything to happen just as it did. I want to bottle the joy and closeness. I want to put those beautiful faces in a finely woven basket next to my bed where I can regularly catch a glimpse of their beauty again. I want to look at them at midnight and first thing in the morning. It went too fast, and I long to repeat every second. It reminds me of being with a marvelous and sensitive lover who after a long night of passion leaves too quickly in the morning. I want that feeling of wealth back again. I want to see those beautiful, happy, smiling faces—so proud of what they pulled off, looking at me with deep respect. The event left its mark. We were reminded that our family was not an institution but a finely woven pattern of relationships and the ideal place to cultivate the silent, deep river that flows within.

Making it happen took massive organizing around time, place, food, activities, schedules, money, sleeping accommodations, work constraints, child care, dozens of e-mails and telephone calls, strategizing about pick-ups and drop-offs, and of course, it took massive faith they could make it happen. I do know that sweet love and honest intent was behind the propulsion of the energy.

They came to Palm Springs, California, from all over the country so they could speak the words that are usually spoken at a eulogy. It was clear they wanted me to understand the contribution I had made to their lives. They were, of course, also taking care of themselves by expressing their gratitude to me. It showed self-generosity, vulnerability, and a willingness to do the right thing for the right reason. The decision that each made in order for this event to occur was not lost on me. A big story was being written. It was a story that cannot be altered, edited, or taken back. It happened. It happened to us, and we were all changed by it. We grew and we loved. It was far more than music to this mother's ears. With all their complexities, strength, and humanness, my children wrote into my legacy profound moments of healing this mother's heart. Long after I am gone, I hope they will be in awe of themselves and the events that transpired over those four days in Palm Springs, California.

We spent our time talking nonstop, laughing, cooking, eating, swimming, and exercising. We floated for hours on end on colorful rubber mats in the swimming pool. We floated over to this person and then floated over to another. We offered comfort to anyone in need of healing; we offered our own experience, compassion, understanding, expertise, intense listening, and lots of advice to each other. Lots of advice. On Saturday night we gathered for a beautiful meal. They set a plastic crown on my white hair and gave me a magic wand. Then, one by one, each rose to read their prepared tribute to me. I was dumbstruck and cried in disbelief, thankfulness, and awe. I cried from wonder and amazement, and I praised our shared experience. I cried full, deep, belly tears for all the world's mothers who thought they did not do enough, were not smart enough, not intuitive enough, were not fortune-tellers and mathematicians. My family and I have a story to tell about that night, we have tears to remember and profound gratefulness to carry us along when life unexpectedly separates us and we wish we were back in Palm Springs floating around on colorful rubber mats.

In retrospect, life was so simple when the children were small and the world we lived in was small. There was a time when they gave me all the kisses and hugs a mother could want. Their demands were, in the broad sense, quite manageable. They were still uncomplicated, delighted being in my company, and accepted my every word as gospel. Yes, it was an easier time. Focus was clear and the task was unmistakable. And as the years passed and they naturally grew to develop lives of their own, I too elected to expand my sense of place to include environments that had little to do with my family. I enrolled in college, graduated after eight years, and went into the job market where my creativity was placed on helping other people prosper. My loyalties were divided, and though I struggled day and night to accept the breakdown of my time and labor, guilt followed me like a shadow.

The truth was a sweet and wholesome era was gone. Huge sewing projects were over, baking blueberry muffins and dozens of tea rings to be given as Christmas gifts were over. Things had shifted. The great story of the universe was being enacted before me and in me. Maturation, loss, and increase were everywhere, following a course that has driven people throughout human history. The combination of living with the inevitability of children growing up and the awakening of my own potential, although right and just, lived in me as a punishing phantom, and I could not get out of its clutches. An overarching guilt turned everything into a contest between being at home or being at the office. It turned an early evening meeting with the dean into a feeling that I was committing a crime. The competing urgencies of my life were at constant war. Intellectually, I knew that being true to oneself was a charge we are all given at birth, but motherhood makes things murky. When it comes to motherhood, there is no one size fits all. We can talk all day about quality time with our children and our obligation to be true to our own needs. But at the end of the day, a mother is either at home or she is not.

My vote is for women and their resourcefulness. I cheer the mother who can be true to herself and make peaceful closure at the end of each day, no matter what she chooses.

Enormous research has gone into trying to understand what makes mothers tick. But the human instinct to love does not stand up well to a flow chart. I suggest we each do the best we can and accept ourselves as a mystery in a world that loves answers. That should be enough.

Wisdom Lesson

There comes a time when a mother must let go of her children and take her place as an elder.

It is imperative that a woman makes peace with her motherhood.

It takes inner strength, and there is nothing easy about it. It requires intention and stamina to come to terms with those early years when many of us were flying by the seat of our pants about serious issues that required discernment and information. But in my generation, there was no information. Dr. Spock was it. Dr. Spock and his two-six-ten feedings.

Many of us did not know what we were doing. We were not old enough to know how to handle our own lives well, much less handle the tender lives of those in our care. We all recall times when we were unsupported emotionally and financially, when we wrestled with night feedings, schedules, exhaustion, lack of privacy, fussy eaters, report cards, bad teachers and wonderful teachers, health insurance, hygiene issues, food budgets and eating habits, setting curfews, dating appropriateness, sex education, homework, our children's friendships and our own, allowances, houses that were too small and some that where too large, competition among children, and competition among other mothers, gossip about husbands, sleepless nights, our envy of a curvaceous mother, when to let go of our children or when to hang on for dear life.

But for every one thing that was a struggle there were two that were life-enhancing, making us better people in the long run.

I want to tell all mothers to forgive themselves. Those who have ever worried themselves sick about their children and felt alone in the middle of the night, "You do not have to walk on broken glass for the rest of your life, repenting for not being perfect." It is time to let go.

Come out of the guilt closet. Feel your beauty, realize what you have been through, be honest about how you wished you knew then what you know now. Put on your yellow silk dress with its fifteen pearl buttons, pin a gardenia in your hair, and make a visit to church. Stop in the park to feed the ducks, go home and open the widows wide so the neighbors will hear you whistle "Over the Rainbow." Rejoice you are still alive to tell the story. Slip into your red satin nightgown as the day fades and dance to Beethoven's "Moonlight Sonata." Call your children. Tell them you are grateful to be their mother. In the morning, walk down Broadway while wearing your best lavender hat. Praise your reflection in the store windows, wave at all the taxi drivers, and smile at their shouts of praise. You deserve it.

It is never too late to learn how to be fabulous.

THE POWDER-BLUE BATHING SUIT: FEAR OF BEING FABULOUS

Beauty is my real aim.—Gandhi

When I was eighteen, a photographer asked if I would be willing to pose for him.

I was sunning myself in my new powder-blue bathing suit by the side of Olympic Park pool when a handsome young man sat down on his towel close to mine. Soon we were engaged in conversation. I would like to say that one subject led to another, but I was not conversant enough to have a lot to talk about. In contrast, he seemed very self-confident. He was handsome, appealing, and unlike any man I had met. I had seen more than my share of pain and was unconscious of my own beauty and feminine power. I didn't understand why he sat next to me in the first place.

After a time he asked if he might photograph me. He had a studio not far from where we sat, and he said he would be honored to take my picture. Instantly, I was threatened and overwhelmed. Anything unfamiliar had the power to shut me down. His was an invitation to add something new to my very short resume of worldly adventures.

As soon as he posed his question, I put a wall between us that ensured our easy conversation would quickly end. My deeply entrenched fear of standing out or being special in any way paralyzed me. I simply could not hear that he was recognizing me as a pretty young woman. Saying yes required a courage and openness I did not yet have. I might have given him the impression that I was accessible because I laughed and smiled a lot. But that was a cover for a complete lack of self-confidence and a fear of standing out. Being considered noteworthy enough to be photographed was far more than I could deal with. The truth was the conversation had taken a turn that asked far more than I could deliver. So I said, "I am not interested. No, I could not possibly do that. Anyway, I am getting married in September."

Feeling embarrassed and awkward, I dove into the pool, swam out twenty yards, realizing in a flash that I regretted my answer. I had made a terrible mistake. For a moment, I had convinced myself that life was just dandy as it was. The truth was my life was anything but dandy. It was monotonous, flat, bland, predictable, and lacked inspiration of any kind. A psychology of personal growth had not yet presented itself at my doorstep, and it would be many years before I garnered enough experience to graciously accept acknowledgement of any kind. My automatic response to the risky possibility of spreading my wings was to shut down.

I will never know if the dark-haired photographer had any motive other than to photograph me. What was certain, however, is that fear of doing anything outside the range of my normal activity terrified me, and being the target of the young photographer's attention sent me into a panic. The possibility that he might have interest in me beyond the camera was more than this eighteen-year-old could manage. I could not think or choose. I could only react. Making healthy choices in regard to my needs and wishes would be years down the road. That the situation held a taint of sexual appeal made it all the more threatening. The real truth was I was not afraid of him as much as I was afraid of myself.

In a panic I turned around and rapidly swam the twenty yards back to where the photographer had been sitting. But the photographer and his towel were gone. It was as if the exchange had never happened. He simply vanished, like a genie that had momentarily escaped from his bottle to offer a magic elixir only to quickly disappear inside it again. I searched the entire pool area, but there was no sign of him. I stood for a long time outside the men's exit, hoping to catch a glimpse of him. I went back the next day and sat on the same towel, in the same place, wearing my powder-blue bathing suit. But he never came back. I felt like a disappointed bride waiting at the altar for a groom that never materialized. The memory of the experience is as alive as if it had happened yesterday. I can still see the dark-haired photographer and myself sitting side by side near the edge of the swimming pool. I still see him looking at me with his dark-brown eyes and remember how close his towel was to mine. There was nothing in my experience that remotely hinted at my being distinguished in any way, and I could not walk into his offer. The psychological defenses I erected to keep me safe turned instead to cement walls that kept other people and their new ideas out. I was blocked from having my own experience, and it would be many years before I could believe that the word *self-esteem* had anything whatsoever to do with me. When I finally did hear that word spoken by someone that I respected, I was forty-four years old.

The day came when I slowly unearthed my family history. It was a relief to name the cause of my troubling inclination to hide from any action suggesting I was special. Being chosen made me feel unsafe. In the family I came from, being a pretty girl was not considered to be of value. On the contrary, our family had secrets and we had shame. The deeply entrenched problems of my parents were more hardcore and immediate than any soft notion of photographing my pretty face.

In the years following my experience with the photographer, I did what we all do. I moved on as best I could. Beautiful things happened to me and terrible things happened to me. But year by year, I rose to breathe in the liberating feeling of self-worth, and I slowly understood that if I respected myself, I would be able to accept all praise with a spirit of simple and pure gratitude.

The photographer and his offer have visited my thoughts over the years, and I will never know what would have happened had I stepped out of my small world to embrace the world he represented. What is certain is that his attention was impossible to receive. Stepping out of my fear-based reality was not remotely possible. I could not risk, change, and grow. All I could do was turn and run.

The photographer offered the magic potion of broadening my horizons. I just was not ready for it. I am still trying to forgive myself.

Wisdom Lesson

Love yourself through all the regrets and missed opportunities—the "wish-I-hads and the if-onlys.

The above story drives home two lessons: we must learn to receive, and we must do the careful work of self-acceptance. Not one woman who wishes to age beautifully is exempt from understanding the complexities of these lessons.

Beauty is a charged word. It can separate us from one another by hitting our comparison buttons. Here is where a beauty conversation is beneficial. We need to talk about the tender subject of beauty. We cannot change anyone's face or body, but that is not the goal. The goal is protect and nurture our beauty.

I propose a national beauty conversation. Everyone will be invited to participate: movie stars, TV producers, models, the titans of fashion, athletes, dancers, pediatricians, teachers, health advocates, financiers, publishing houses, politicians, students from kindergarten to PhDs, and the movers and shakers in the marketing industry. The mission will be twofold:

(1) to reach a more inclusive definition of beauty

(2) to understand the way beauty exhibits itself in our daily lives.

Several years ago I conducted a random survey with women from ages eighteen to seventy-one. The summation was: women feel beautiful when they are happy, confident, sexy, and alive. When asked, "What kind of an older woman do you want to be," most women stated they wanted to be compassionate, wise, healthy, graceful, and generous. When asked about role models, most women named Mother Teresa.

No matter what the age of the woman filling out the survey, Mother Teresa was considered to be beautiful. We have all observed her well-lined face brimming with love and compassion for the sick and poor, the disinherited and disenfranchised. There could be no doubt she was solidly focused in her intention to bring comfort to the downtrodden. Mother Teresa *connected,* and we felt that we knew her. We didn't need to know the details, but we knew goodness and beauty when we saw it. In some unexplainable way, Mother Teresa made us feel better about ourselves. She was an example of power, vulnerability, and the strengthened heart. True beauty is like that. It is inspiring and uplifting. Great art often leaves us speechless. Music, theatre, and star performances in sports help us to know the heights to which a human being can rise. We follow these folks around the world to watch them perform. We rise to our feet when a star athlete does the impossible. We might be couch potatoes ourselves; nonetheless, we identify with the indescribable something that sparks some to higher levels of being. Mother Teresa offered an example of beauty, leaving us with a lot to admire. She always came into the room empty.

My friend and drama therapist, Henry, works with Alzheimer's patients, teasing out brief moments of memory, getting people who have lost the capacity to respond to respond. I have seen Henry kneel like a lover about to propose beside the wheelchair of a woman who seemed lost to the world. I have observed him lift the invisible veil that separates her from active society through his uncanny ability to communicate in a way that defies explanation. And while the patient's contact with the present was brief, and she soon dropped back into her lost world, it was nonetheless real for a time. I never observed this action without marveling at the compassion and tenderness that was on display. One could never witness one person's affinity to another on this high level without being moved. What I observed was one man's ability to be in empathetic relationship with those grappling to simply get through the moment. He was a human being demonstrating our oneness, and it was beautiful to behold. At those times, Henry came into the room empty.

For years, I had a photograph of Brandi Chastain hanging in my studio. It was shot as she fell to her knees after she made the penalty kick in the Women's World Cup 1999. She pulled off her top jersey to the roar of thousands. That roar came from our recognition of her fierce dedication, unwavering belief in the task, and the raw talent on display. Brandi was the beauty conversation coming onto the field empty.

One might not think that a nun, an athlete, and a drama therapist have much in common, but they are cut from the same cloth. They exhibit a natural feel for grace and grit, the discipline to stay the course, and an ability to connect with their fellow man. All three are the real deal. They reach into themselves and pull out the magic that lifts us all up. Greatness is a phenomenon we resonate with because we all have greatness in ourselves.

There are millions of beautiful people whose photographs do not make the cover of a magazine. The shape-shifter mother who still nurtures her children after a hard day at the office, the eighty-year-old getting a bachelor's degree in mathematics; the introvert taking a class on stripping for her lover.

A childhood friend recently sent me a Christmas card with the note, "Hope you are doing well. Many years since we first met at Chancellor Avenue grade school! I don't know about you, but that girl still lives in me—just more wise." Her expression was the beauty conversation coming in a Christmas card. My old grade school friend still feels beautiful as she walks around in her seventy-five-year-old body. She has the healthy ego to let go and appreciate herself for who she is today.

The national beauty conversation survey listed below will help you focus on what beauty and aging mean to you. When you have completed the survey, share your answers with others to get their opinions and points of view.

> The beauty conversation includes the principles of blessing, inclusion, grace, and praise, and all women who yearn for a new conversation on aging and beauty find themselves identifying with these words. Old women, young women, short, tall, fat, thin, balding, those wearing makeup and those that shun it completely, stay-at-home moms and working moms, single, married, widowed, divorced, gay and bisexual, educated women, women who have had cosmetic surgery and women who mock them, women who lack formal education, money-rich women and women who are rich without a penny in the a bank. From this point forward, the beauty conversation has hit its stride. And we are all taking our rightful place as an archetype of wisdom, beauty, and moral influence.

The task is to stand as one voice in a national beauty conversation. Let us not be daunted by our determination to shift the country's obsession with youth. While our task is huge, so is our intention. The simultaneous occurrence of unprecedented worldwide change and forty-five million women collecting Social Security is a forceful mix feeding and supporting the transformation of human values. The importance of acknowledging the titanic power inherent in the aging process as a planetary change agent in and of itself must not be underestimated. It must be harnessed and brought to front stage.

The vision to change the cultural conversation on aging and beauty is ours for the taking. We need not get caught in the details of how this paradigm shift is going to occur. Vision rarely starts with the details.

I encourage you to give yourself over to the powerful declaration: "Aging is not my enemy, aging can be my ally."

Making this declaration regularly empowers you to see getting older as a creative opportunity to be hip, honest, full-bodied, informed, savvy, and conspicuous. You bring wisdom, experience, and audacity. The millions of women who will join in the national beauty conversation will have this declaration on their lips, and it will fill the air that we breathe. *Aging is my ally* is the ultimate beauty cry running counter to the current aging mantra that spawns fear and separation. (BTW, this is a tee shirt waiting to happen!) *Aging is my ally* is a compassionate response to the life you have lived and the world you want to leave your sons and daughters. Make no mistake about it, we will not only be changing women's hearts and minds, we will be changing generations. A point of caution: as we go through this evolution, not one of us is absolved of the daily responsibility of taking care of our bodies. Exercising regularly and eating correctly will be more important than ever because we need our strength—physical, intellectual, and spiritual.

Trust that all manner of things will fall into place once the national beauty conversation hits the airways. But let's not march ahead; let's dance forward with justice as our dance partner. This is a call for the good news.

The national beauty conversation survey focuses on what beauty and aging mean to you and how they influence your life. Your answers will be the beauty threads flowing organically into your conversations.

1. What three words describe you when you are really feeling beautiful?
2. Do you believe that true beauty is about inner beauty?
3. If yes, what causes you to forget this from time to time?
4. Do you ever think of compassion and presence as representing beauty?
5. If yes, name two women who fit that description.
6. What do they look like?
7. How does your perception of beauty affect your career?

8. Do you know women who you consider role models?
9. What three qualities stand out in them?
10. How did/are your parents aging?
11. Are you able to shut out the messages promoted by the majority of the media?
12. Please explain how you do that.
13. Do you have a support system that shares your views?
14. What three adjectives describe the older woman you want to be?
15. Do you ever waiver in your answers to the previous question?
16. Do you want to join the national beauty conversation?
17. What may be lost by doing this?
18. What do you bring to the conversation?
19. What is your deepest hope for a national beauty conversation?

PART III

BRING MEANING INTO YOUR LIFE

"All the hazards of life are elements out of which we can fashion whatever we like."—Novalis in *Original Blessing* by Matthew Fox

THE PINK CHRYSLER

Our legacy defines us. It underscores what we valued and gives meaning to the years when we walked the earth.

I don't recall exactly when my father bought the old Chrysler. I only remember it was pink, massive in size, and heavily adorned inside and out with chrome. It had an in-your-face obviousness that is usually reserved for wedding cakes and gingerbread houses. It was a tank of a car, a 1960 fortress with huge whitewall tires, a push-button mounted on the steering column, and comfortable plaid couches, front and back. It was the podium from which, for eighteen years and 900 Sunday visits, my father faithfully visited my mother.

Some might call it vulgar and tasteless, but my father loved that car. The pink Chrysler transformed a feeling of having no special place that he and Ellen Gertrude could call their own to having something that was their place alone, a sort of traveling home that brought a sense of respectability to their Sunday visits. The old car became a table of plenty delivering little episodes of freedom that temporarily interrupted my mother's life as an outcast. It was a haven in common leading her from the bowels of mind-numbing, undeviating change to the blessed relief of not being on exhibition. Whatever limits bound the marriage, the car became God's great communion rail and a sweep of the universe itself. It hardly mattered that they looked like lonely troopers on life's highway. The truth was they had carved out a place for themselves where they kept a feast that few understood. My father, Arthur Edward, and my mother, Ellen Gertrude, were in this together. The illness targeted the life of Ellen Gertrude, but Arthur Edward also felt the blows. Sometimes he was just a mess, a man coming apart at the seams, bitter and resentful of the limits placed on him. He was trapped because he would not desert her. His inner code would not allow it. Without this code he could have made the decision to walk away. He could have cut the cord and that would have been the end of it. But there were consequences whatever he chose, and he chose to stand with her. He never wavered from his choice and this would remain consistently true until the end. Everything came in increments. Bits of beauty filtering down into his life, offering a reprieve here and a reprieve there. He became an expert on increments. He could pick it up and put it down. Pick it up and put it down. He was an early expert on stress management.

She had a habit of calling out his name, "Arthur, Arthur." I heard it a thousand times, and I can still hear it. It was the sound of terror and pleading. Everything they encountered was a part of their epic journey. They were riding the arc of heaven where for millennia the universal story of chaos and beauty is written.

I was twenty-eight years old and a mother of two little girls, operating in a world of sewing machines, organdy pinafores, and perfect apple pies when my mother was committed, and the big hospital with its many locked doors and unhappy people could overwhelm me. But when I joined my father for a Sunday visit and the three of us climbed into the Chrysler, an engagement of a different kind took place. There was no hiding. We were on our own. The sharpness of commitment, the gravity of illness, ancient memories recalling the grapes of the marriage bed, the knowledge that Ellen Gertrude would be returning to the Unpredictables at 5:00 p.m. and my father and I were going home—everything was amplified tenfold. But if the Chrysler could have talked, it might have said, "The human instinct to press on is bigger than the blood draining out." Somehow my mother and father knew how to nurture the heart after it had been cracked open, bled dry, and left for dead. Their little traveling home brought happiness in increments. It was calculated and fleeting, but just enough to let them know the disease that took her mental health had not stolen every scrap of distinctiveness and definition from our little family. It was sobering to understand that happiness coming only in increments is sustainable. Sometimes, it is enough.

Before my eyes, a soulful story of redemption was in the making. It was a story that put flesh on compassion. In that place, we constructed a story defining the sacredness of witness, the grace of listening, the paradox of simultaneous involvement and detachment. The story is all. It builds our emotional bones. My parents' story informed my life on many levels and continues to bless generations of children, grandchildren, and great-grandchildren. It has been decades since the passing of my parents, but when I recall those Sunday visits I realize they left me a superlative example of endurance, loyalty, and commitment.

In the beginning of their marriage they were lusty in love, and it never mattered that money was in short supply. But eight years into the marriage, she fell into the clutches of an all-enveloping illness that brought with it repetitive, emotional, financial, and physical stress. They were stretched to the limit in every circumstance. The haphazard nature of her epileptic seizures made her a pariah at social events, and gradually she was not welcome at family gatherings. Yet my parents' original attachment, so passionately felt in the early dynamic, appeared to continue in some mysterious alchemy.

With the early, dire prognoses from the medical profession, Arthur Edward and Ellen Gertrude formed a united resolve to work at keeping her seizures in some kind of manageable state for as long as possible. It was the first of many soulful junctures where a decision had to be made. They decided to pitch their tent on the banks of hope. They would count the days between seizures, thrilled when ten days went by without one, and then hit the rocks of despair when the thief that was stealing their lives broke in without warning, traumatizing everyone and sending her, totally exhausted, to bed. The story of beauty and chaos had begun and there was no stopping its advance. But my mother and father fed each other a pungent yes to the commitment of continuing on.

Neither of them could have foreseen the breeding ground of family violence that years of ostracism, shame, and mental deterioration would set in place. My parents were not formally educated people. They were good, sweet people. How could they possibly know the future would bring stormy nights when they would scarcely recognize themselves. A vicious spiral of tension could unleash demeaning accusations toward each other that traumatized each deeply. At these moments, they were like screaming, hysterical babies in need of soothing and love. After one of these exhausting episodes, Mrs. Beardsley, a downstairs neighbor and RN, came upstairs to see if she could help. But there was nothing anyone could do. The circumstances had a life of their own and despair easily set in after one of these outbursts. They were heading into unchartered territory with little support from outsiders; in retrospect, it was a merciful thing they did not know how deep their wounds would go or that it would continue for thirty-six more years. Friends and neighbors vanished, no one felt safe around her. No one wanted to be near a woman who could, without warning, collapse in violent convulsions and in a semi stupor ask her children who they were.

In the beginning, when the demon illness was in its initial stage, Ellen Gertrude was able to manage their simple, cold-water flat without too much difficulty. There were still evenings when sensuality filled the air, allowing husband and wife to experience the joy of attraction. The sexual appeal that drew them together in the first place had not diminished at all. He would pull out the old harmonica, throw his head back, violently tap his foot to a rich tempo, and encourage Ellen Gertrude to raise her cotton housedress to the thigh and kick her beautiful, thin, smooth-skinned legs into the air and tap dance on the red-and-white linoleum floor. Her blue eyes sparkled and her thick, blonde hair framed a face aglow with robust energy and good health. No one could possibility doubt that she was anything other than a beautiful, lucid, sexual woman. Those were the times of happiness that Arthur Edward tucked away on the shelves of his mind. Perhaps the memory of her, vivacious and still full with giving, sustained him when the tempest broke in all its fury. Continuing to make music would have been a very good thing for them both, but there came a day when the old harmonica stayed in the drawer. There was no place for it anymore. He was exhausted, and music was the last thing on his mind.

Over the years, I grew to appreciate my father's car for many reasons, but one that stands out is that it was in the backseat of the old, pink Chrysler that I learned to listen. Sitting in the backseat listening to him listen to her was an experience in listening that cannot be replicated through didactic means. The finest teacher will never be able to directly communicate the nuances, pauses, silences, responses, and poetry that go into listening beautifully. My father modeled the skill, and to this day, I make my living listening. The times I joined them on their Sunday drive, I heard banter about the weather, his dead-end job, the rotten Republicans and crazy Democrats, the high cost of things, and about Violet, the sister who never once, in eighteen years, came to visit. I heard complaining and nagging, fear and hysteria. I heard pleading and begging, "Arthur, Arthur, why can't I come home?" The question was most often met with silence, but it was, for me, the beginning of a lifelong understanding that sometimes there are hard questions that defy easy answers.

Describing the place the Chrysler had in our lives evokes vivid memories of Arthur Edward, and sometimes, me, exiting the highway shortly before 1:00 p. m. to travel the last few miles to Matthew Hospital for the Mentally Ill. He pulls into the small, near-empty visitor's parking lot. I remain in the car as he walks to the familiar red-brick building, the one that houses the select group of patients that are identified as "Unpredictables." He rings the bell, waits. Soon a pleasant-looking nurse unlocks the door. It is clear she is expecting him. His reputation for loyalty is well-known to the staff. The nurse and my father work together like those who bond in a delivery room. They have a tacit agreement to protect Ellen Gertrude—she by detaining my mother inside the human warehouse, and he by delivering her into the sun once a week. Shortly my parents emerge, and Ellen Gertrude's bright red coat with its big, shiny, black buttons stand in sharp contrast to this colorless place. She is outside now, but we all know that she will forever be inside. It is immediately evident what kind of a day it will be by the expression on Mother's face. The tone of our visit begins the moment we catch sight of her mood, and each of us will instinctively decide on the best defense posture to take. No alleluia chorus greets us here. We are making our way over broken glass. Mother must be back in the ward by 5:00 p.m., so we hurry on.

Slowly, my father steers the car out of the parking lot and onto the open road. About midway through the afternoon he locates a spot that will avail us some privacy. He pulls of the road, parks, and begins the ritual presentation of food, candy, industrial strength paper towels, coffee, two paperback mystery novels, and cigarettes. In eighteen years her preferences will never change. Two roast beef sandwiches with mayonnaise on soft, white bread, a thermos of very strong coffee heavily laced with sugar, seven packs of cherry Life Savers bound with three rubber bands, and four packs of Camel cigarettes. Sitting in the old Chrysler, the place that gives her privacy and the feeling she is a normal part of society, she draws in the nicotine with the same ferocious energy that she applies to draining the thermos. She can't seem to get enough sugar or enough smoke. Her fingers and nails tell the story of a woman who has held thousands of burning cigarettes. Once entering the Chrysler, she smokes without stop.

I wince uneasily as my mind flashes back on early childhood images of her once beautiful, unstained hands making me pink flannel petticoats trimmed with blue crocheting around the neckline. Beautiful hands combing my hair and putting huge, three-inch-wide blue ribbons atop my blonde head. Beautiful hands placing pajamas with rubber buttons on the hot radiator so that they would be warm when she slips me into them at bedtime. Back then, she was tender and protective in the extreme.

But what is of crucial significance is that in the interminable suffering of my beloved mother and the depth of understanding and devotion of my father is the birth of, and handing down of, a powerful family story. The pain living in the family embossed forbearance on our souls, carried medicine that created us, stamped us with a fervor for understanding, turned bloodletting into an entire sequence of transformations that continues to give shape and identity to everything that has existed for generations. Their love slowly, but definitely, eroded during the eighteen years leading up to her confinement. What took its place was a deep level of care and concern that rendered a grace to a marriage that had gone far, far afield from its original coupling. Their lives reflected disruption and order, chaos and beauty, fury and touching moments of sweetness. And as well, their lives bore the evidence of staying the course. It hardly mattered that they looked like lonely troopers on God's highway; they had carved out a niche for themselves and the Devil be dammed.

Layer upon layer of relatedness swam within the confines of the pink Chrysler. Afternoons when neither of them could convey the range of their anger and resentment and they sat in heavy silence within a cloud of thick cigarette smoke. Hours when Arthur Edward listened attentively and responded thoughtfully to all her questions and observations without ever being condescending or patronizing. The Sundays when heightened tensions grew between them because a New Jersey winter snowstorm made driving treacherous. The devastating feeling that hit him like the wrath of God if the roast beef was tough or when he could not find cherry Life Savers in his local store and dared substitute another flavor! Or when he simply used two rubbers bands instead of three to wrap the Life Savers together and all hell broke loose. And then there were the times when there rose from Ellen Gertrude glimpses of her old self. She would talk about feeling protective of another patient or reported good progress in the making of potholders and cotton aprons for the annual hospital bazaar.

Many times over the years Arthur Edward was questioned by his friends, coworkers, his sister, Hazel, hospital staff, as well as me as to how he remained so consistently devoted to a woman who demanded so much and appeared to give so little in return. He never gave a clear answer. But he never thought of himself as a victim and always knew that while my mother was not free to choose where and how she lived, his choices were many. At no time did he lose sight of the fact that he could quit his uninspiring and thankless job at the insurance company, pack up his small, three-room apartment, leave the state, and start a life somewhere else. Many times, when a Sunday afternoon became four hours of living hell, he found the thoughts of the sunny Florida beaches very tempting. Instead, I watched him make, over and over again, an unequivocal commitment to alleviating in whatever small measure the suffering and monotony of his wife's life. Our hearts admired his tenacity in staying the course. But our minds could not understand. Everyone had a suggestion for a way out of his dilemma, a way to circumvent commitment, a way to justify a retreat from the multilevel obligations that wrapped around his life. However, those who were able to put their own projections aside found they had stumbled on the rare privilege of witnessing one man's long journey to redeem a bereft and heartrending story.

My father was not a saint, nor was he a bleeding heart. He was basically a simple man making his way in a staggeringly complex world. He left a legacy of goodness he would never have been willing to take credit for. There was no doubt he led a life of great meaning.

The part the old car played in our family history was not apparent to me when we were living through it. It is only the passage of time that has allowed me to see the place the car had in creating a family legacy of protection, loyalty, and commitment. Nothing was more important than routinely breaking the rounds of segregation and disempowerment that marked Ellen Gertrude's life. But the Chrysler promised a four-hour respite from these serpents and, by and large, delivered every time.

My life was shaped by this story. Each telling blesses me, polishes my hopes, releases any dark shadows lurking about, waters the seeds of legacy, and unfurls faith in human nature high over my head. It unfailingly brings me to the wisdom question, "What is really important?"

I believe my father was a profoundly spiritual man who had attained a deep wisdom through the endurance of profound grief. He unerringly embodied the meaning of being responsible for another person. He understood that he and only he in all the world could provide my mother the consistent Sunday redemption that was needed. He knew the four-hour reprieve made a difference in her colorless life that was far out of proportion to the actual hours spent driving around in his old Chrysler.

What the two of them really had together we will never really know. The best things are often hard to describe. But I suspect it was the sum of the memory of Harry's on a Saturday night, tap dancing on a red-and-white linoleum floor, roast beef sandwiches heavily spread with mayonnaise, dresses with pockets, Sunday afternoons, and a pink car searching the back roads for a sense of place.

When my father died, blessedly in his sleep at age sixty-five, he was found by his neighbors lying naked in bed with a white sheet pulled up to his shoulders, his right hand on his heart and his left by his side. On the night table was a thick medical book open to a page explaining in detail a coronary. Lying atop the page were his reading glasses. He was telling us that he suspected he was having a heart attack, elected not to alert his friends in the next apartment, and chose in full consciousness to lie down and simply trust the process.

He had made his last decision. No intensive care unit for him. Arthur Edward had had enough of hospitals.

Wisdom Lesson

When we are conscious of the legacy we wish to leave, we act accordingly. Every step of the process opens us to a life commensurate with aging beautifully.

The finest way for any of us to age beautifully is to give serious thought to fashioning a life with meaning.

Legacy is fair. The evidence of your life is your legacy. We each will leave a legacy. In the context of aging beautifully, what would you like your legacy to be? Let us be clear; we are going to leave behind how we have lived. Few will be remembered for their moisturizer.

The thing that will leave everyone in awe long after we have left the earth will be our willingness to follow our dreams all the way to the end, the commitment to doing our best, and our never ending search for the seeds of wisdom.

Preparing yourself for your legacy takes spiritual valor. Electing to go through life choosing the grace notes of forgiveness, self-respect, and honesty is to leave all who witness that behavior a model-worthy replication. Some are daunted by the thoughts of their own legacy. We might even feel that everything we contributed to life will be overshadowed by our shortcomings. The opposite is true. Examining our legacies is a beautiful opportunity to make peace with ourselves by putting old skeletons to rest. By looking at what we will leave behind, we might find that our lives were richer than we thought.

Take heart in knowing that devotion to protecting your beauty is a legacy in itself.

Three tasks are recommended:

* One, consider the great experiences of your life. Not just those that brought you joy, but those that emptied you. Write down what you learned from the experience of recalling them.
* Two, make a list of the *major* transitions you have made over a lifetime. List the strengths that each transition required.
* Three, make a list of what you want to be remembered for.

THIS IS WHERE I CAME TO HEAL

It is never a mistake to search for what one wants. Never.—Clarissa Pinkola Estes

The place I cling to is my second-floor apartment. It is where the walls seem to hear me and twenty-six full-length windows present the afternoon sun. Here is where Ralph Lauren sheets and flesh-tone silk pillowcases caress my tired bones at the end of the day. It is twenty-six steps up to this place where I sleep, work, love, and dream. These six rooms are rooted in a blessed, glorious privacy that I had never before experienced.

I moved in when I was fifty-four and began making my second floor into a personal monastery by filling it with grace and beautiful people who came and went. The lovely walls stand like ten-foot silenced mummies, going from flesh to mauve as the day deepens. The walls are luscious in the daylight and from their west exposure settle into warmth at night. Black lampshades hover over low-set light, and the leopard chaise in the corner waits for someone to take up residence. I have seen pedestrians look up at the big windows, and I imagine them wondering what's going on up here.

My rooms have a voice that speaks to me regularly. The voice is a mother's voice, soft and safe. With mother's arms holding me lovingly yet loosely enough to let me be. Of course, that is what healthy mothers are like. But sometimes things go terribly wrong, and the mother finds she is the one who needs protection from life's slings and arrows. If she is wounded deeply in body, mind, and soul, she becomes incapable of compassionate action toward her own young. She might love her child, but that love does not get translated into protection of her young because she needs protection herself. When a mother is overwhelmed and engulfed by her own pain, she cannot grant her young that first, great imperative—*safety*. The mother needs safety, and no emotional shelter is left for the child. If that calamity occurs and the mother/child rolls get reversed, there is a build-up of grief all around. It can get lodged in the child's lungs for a very long time, taking up crucial, psychic space for the development of self-esteem. Her early childhood development is thwarted, and the child feels shunned and silenced in some very primitive way. She is a child in need of caretaking, and often she is the child *doing* the caretaking.

I was that child. I spent my early adulthood unaware of the price I paid for being raised by a hurting mother. It was not until I was in my fifties that I began to unravel the reasons I had such a fierce need to protect myself and why I clung so desperately to the quiet security of my own company.

But now, my monastery tells me, "I am home, I am safe." Like two pockets sewn into the side seams of a dress, these rooms give me a sense of place. I find meaning here and joyfully share my place with others so they too can feel the honey-sweetness of God.

This second-floor apartment is saturated with tales of love and real-life stories because humanity comes through here. For many years, I conducted men's and women's support groups in this good space. People take twenty-six steps up to talk and spin tales, to grieve broken hearts and broken dreams, to support one another through career transitions and to welcome the magical child within. Their commitment to personal growth always leaves me with a feeling of appreciation for their willingness to trust me, and as the last person closes the door behind them, I look forward to the time when I hear these sweet and treasured people laughing and talking on their way back up here again. I can still feel them long after I wash their emptied teacups and scrape the Trader Joe's cookie crumbs from the table.

My second-floor apartment holds it all. It's where I acknowledged the massive feelings of relief that came after long years of responsibility and too much multitasking and accommodation and embraced instead a blessed life of peace, privacy when I preferred it, and predictable Sundays afternoons in a city bustling with happy people enjoying the sites. I read about rich folks with obscenely large houses and their state-of-the-art burglar alarm systems, celebrities who spend like kings and popes using unlimited credit to buy five cars but can't even drive to Walgreen's to buy deodorant and Kleenex without getting all dolled up. Their complex, wealthy lives have nothing over me. Real wealth is an amalgam of the ability to choose and being able to see the beauty in the madness of it all.

I am quiet here. I can read my books and watch Charlie Rose. I can stare out the windows at the huge apartment house across the street and imagine all kinds of scenarios happening to the many people living there. I have only to pay my rent and, for another whole month, this is mine. All my life I have volunteered to be endlessly wonderful and to do my best to bring people to peace. But here is where life washed me ashore at age fifty-four, and I find a church with golden spires looking at me from my bedroom window where a four-poster bed draped with eighteen yards of white nylon toile holds me gently at the end of the day. It is jolting to think of my mother lying in her metal bed with its single foam-rubber pillow and surrounded by thirty-nine Unpredictables all lying in their metal beds. And though my mother has been dead for many years, I am still shaken by the comparison of our evolutionary paths.

What I know for sure is that this second-floor apartment is my cloister and sense of place. It looks like I sleep alone, but that is not true. I sleep with gratitude for having found a career so well suited to me. This is where I sleep into myself, steadily recuperating from the demands of the world while wearing a luxurious, red satin nightgown that I wrap around myself to keep my aging body warm.

Wisdom Lesson

A sense of place contributes to aging beautifully by bringing a high level of gratitude into everyday life.

Our sense of place is a unique, very special territory that gives us the feeling of being all of apiece when we are there. Place has our name written all over it. It satisfies the soul, and even ten minutes of place whispers, "You are safe." It does not have to have a specific address, or, as in the above piece, it is a very specific address. Place can be a certain pew in church, a spot along your favorite walk, a seat on the bus, a garden, your side of the bed or your armchair. It is your little corner of the world even if only briefly. It is special. It may be hard to define, yet we know when it is absent.

Place has a special kind of boundary, it is where we belong and where our core pulls us to be. Your place is a territory all its own.

There came a point when my second-floor apartment no longer felt safe. At age seventy-five, the twenty-six marble stairs, once considered a romantic trip to paradise, simply became a treacherous, slow climb and an accident waiting to happen. After a great deal of personal scrutiny and many tearful good-byes with people I had come to love, I moved on. I will always cherish those lovely mauve walls and wide, full-length windows with their western exposure. They were part of what defined me for a period of twenty-one years. I laughed and loved and prayed and established myself as a full-fledged single woman there. I established hundreds of profoundly rich relationships in one of the most beautiful cities on the planet, and it was a stunning experience from start to finish. My memories are the best. San Francisco was the right place at the right time.

My sense of place has changed in the past few years because I have changed. It is now another time with another place. I need to reconsider my energy level, my finances, and the direction of my work as a writer. Everything has changed and nothing has changed. *What was important in San Francisco continues to be important in Eugene, Oregon. And how I see the world* is true wherever I am.

Slowly, I have been creating a new cloister. I have time enough to let self-compassion be in my life and space enough to allow healing tears to flow. It was a surprise to me that I needed to cry. But I find the purging wonderful, and I never dampen my feelings. I rest every day now. Interestingly enough, I don't look in the mirror as often, either.

The jury is out insofar as to my next step. But I am not afraid. I have met redemption on the road to finding myself.

And my red nightgown? I continue to wrap it around me because it keeps me warm. I can almost hear it whisper, "You are safe. You are home wherever you are."

"FOR YOUR AGE..."

When it is over, I want to say: all my life I was a bride married to amazement. I was a bridegroom, taking the world in my arms. I don't want to end up simply having visiting this world.—Mary Oliver

I once lived in a small Southern community where women wore their nightgowns and bathrobes while walking their dogs on a Saturday morning.

The first morning I observed this activity I was rather taken back, but the luxuriousness of feeling this kind of safety was easy to get used to. People stop to talk, invite me in for coffee, everyone says, "Good morning," no one looks away, every breed of dog is represented, and couples in cars wave to neighbors. There is a sizable population of single, older women that suit me. Some are retired, but just as many are still working full time with no immediate plans to give up a full-time schedule. Every person seems happy in this town. I find that nothing short of miraculous! I want to export it all around the world.

One weekend morning, a neighbor on the next cul-de-sac invited me over to see her newly painted light-blue bedroom. The room was quite lovely, and I was happy to share in her accomplishment. One particularly long wall was free of any ornamentation because, as she said, "The wall speaks to a feeling of peace." She spoke from a place of contentment, and it was a delight to be in her company. We were two women taking a reprieve from our Saturday morning tasks to chat about the small things that make a big difference. That she was a nuclear scientist running her own laboratory made it all the more sweet. We spoke for a brief time, chatting about the things many of us talk about—good work and good men, feeling appreciated by our adult children, and the relief we feel when they find happiness for themselves. We spoke of our admiration for the resourcefulness of women; clearly, we were stalwart champions of our own sex, and I was proud this fine woman lived near me. It was a casual interchange packed with substance and gratitude.

Our visit over, we walked to the front door. Standing on the porch in the Saturday morning sunlight, she touched my cheek ever so lightly and said, "You are so beautiful for your age." Of course I knew what she meant. She was trumpeting generosity and sincerely believed she was paying me a compliment. I heard the compliment, but I have to admit that the caveat "for your age" had a jarring ring to it. It felt like a big, red disclaimer plastered to the end of a beautiful tribute. It felt condescending and patronizing, and I didn't like it one bit!

I did not bring this to her attention because I knew she thought she was complimenting me. The fact that the phrase fell so easily from a well-read, highly educated, contemporary woman was unnerving.

Wisdom Lesson

Every woman has the right to be honored for who she is.

There are meaningful lessons here. First, let us not rush to make excuses for all the *genuinely* good women who regularly add the disclaimer to the end of a compliment. I experience these disclaimers coming from women everywhere, and it never ceases to amaze me that we are unaware of the ageist innuendo. At the end of the day, each of us is responsible for the language we use. I don't think we are sufficiently aware of this "for your age" putdown. If we really did hear the less-than-artful subtlety of the tailpiece, I believe we would stop. We are either artful when paying tribute to an older woman or we miss the mark altogether. Directing our thoughts to language is part of the beauty conversation that raises the bar on personal responsibility.

We are addressing a subtle form of discrimination. I am not an overbearing purist, but there is no such thing as a little prejudice. History and habit have a way of settling into social discourse, and the labyrinth of deeply entrenched perceptions are hard to change. They take on a life of their own and then slip from our lips without us even knowing.

My experience tells me there is a very low expectation for older women that even the best and brightest of us do not recognize. We really have a chance to make history. We can turn discrimination on its head. Why was an addendum to the compliment at all necessary? Are we so programmed to think of older women as not being beautiful that it comes as a shock when we see an older woman who is beautiful and thriving as well? When a seventy-five-year-old woman is told, "You are smart and quick for your age," tell me, am I being too sensitive?

Am I on to something so subtle and nuanced that we miss the point of bigotry? David Abram states in *The Art of the Sensuous,* "Whatever we are focused on is what we are in relationship with. Participation is the name of the game." In this story, whether we want to admit it or not, we are participating in a crime against ourselves. Could we please stop discriminating against our own sex? If an older woman exhibits both lust and beauty, why do we discredit her by thinking that lust and beauty is surprising and off the wall for an older woman?

We are cocreators of equality, and we can raise the bar of justice. Not granting each person his or her right to age without subtitles of suspicion is healthy for everyone.

We often define women by what they look like, thereby failing to see the young girl inside that is still roaring to go! Yes, our looks will change. Surely, as night follows day, the way we look will change drastically. It will overtake a woman at some point and possibly throw her into crisis while those on the sidelines stand watching the meltdown. We must renew our vows to honor ourselves and every older woman we meet.

We show our compassion for one another by acknowledging that older women have a beauty all their own. Let's put on our red satin nightgowns and examine our expectations. Let's get past this.

Time to gather our smarts, our wisdom thoughts, and skills in dealing with crisis. We can help our looks with the use of technology, and there is nothing wrong with that. But sooner or later, enough will be enough. Even if we have the best eyelift in the world performed by the best surgeon in the world and the best eye makeup in the world applied by the best makeup artist in the world, there is *something* that says, "This woman has some serious years on her." It is going to be like that for everyone. It is apparent that our changing looks are the Achilles heel of aging beautifully and is core to having an honest beauty conversation.

We must get past our preconceived idea of what older women represent. We need everyone's participation in order to set a new course. So let's call in the poets and rappers. Let's call in Joan of Arc, Abigail Adams, Amelia Earhart, the filthy rich, the desperately poor, the strippers, the pious, the uptight, and the women with walkers. Call in everybody. in particular, call in Ellen Gertrude Mc Mahon and all the women who have felt the wrath of victimization.

Call in Marilyn Monroe. In Gloria Steinman's book, *Marilyn,* Steinem quotes her, "Men expect so much of me because of the image they've made of me as a sex symbol. Men expect so much, and I can't live up to it. They expect bells to ring and whistles to whistle, but my anatomy is the same as any other woman's. I can't live up to it." There is the truth knocking on Marilyn's front door.

BURYING YOURSELF ALIVE IS A DISTINCT OPTION

Nothing so determines who we will become so much as those things we choose to ignore.—Sandor McNab

When I was sixty-nine I received an invitation to my fiftieth high school reunion.

The first question was, "Should I go?" Every woman knows the second question, "What will I wear?" But no matter what I wore, I was not going to look like the young, blonde, skinny, smoothed-skinned girl I was back then. My hair was white, and I had put on thirty pounds since high school. But I had infinitely more confidence and wisdom plus a healthy share of worldly success. So I put on my black leather pants, sucked in my stomach, and with a mixture of excitement, dread, and curiosity, I walked into the lounge of the hotel on that Friday night in Rahway, New Jersey, determined to enjoy myself.

Needless to say, we had all changed a lot. I did not recognize anyone and assumed no one recognized me either. Then from across the room I heard a woman scream, "Ilene McMahon! How *are* you?" I turned to a gray-haired woman I did not recognize but was nonetheless overjoyed to connect with a sister graduate. I greeted her with enthusiasm, and we eagerly did the appropriate information gathering about our current lives. We talked and laughed and shared our intrigue about all the other one hundred and fifty sixty-nine-year-olds filling the lounge. We took a special delight in seeing that the women had aged so much better than the men.

There was something warm and wonderful about it all, and I was glad that I flew the three thousand miles from San Francisco to attend the reunion. Any fears I had conjured up about being uncomfortable simply vanished. The conversation shifted, quite naturally, to our high school days. To our top-ranked football team, split sessions that allowed a lot of us to hold jobs, the bobby socks and saddle shoes, the relative lack of homework, the absence of violence, having our own lockers in the hallway, and of course, we talked about the crushes we had on cute boys. Our eyes danced when we spoke of having the biggest and best marching band in New Jersey. In our mind's eyes we could still see the beautiful flag swingers in their white boots strutting down the field, rain or shine, lighting up all those Saturday afternoons. Fifty years later we were still proud of them. We agreed that life was significantly more innocent back then. No TV, cell phones, or texting. No Facebook, Twitter, or Internet pornography, no MasterCards or movies with sexual content luring teenagers into risky behaviors long before they had gained the discernment to make sound choices. We realized how lucky we were to have had such a wholesome time of it.

Then she said something I will never forget. To this day, her statement sends shivers down my spine. "Oh, those were the best years of our lives!" she blurted out. I stared in shock and disbelief. Somehow I managed to say quietly but with conviction, "They were not the best years of my life. Now is the best time of my life." She hesitated and quietly murmured, "Oh, I wish I could think that." We stood looking at each other as joy was sucked out of the air. There was nothing to be said. It felt awkward and sad, and we each moved on to another fellow graduate and resumed reminiscing.

But the night had ended for me. Here was a lovely woman who had spent fifty years stuck in her youth. I do not believe for a minute that she lacked moments of joy along the way. But thinking that high school presented the best experience that life had to offer tells me that something immeasurably beautiful had stopped for her too early. Had she never held amazement to her breast? Had she never rebelled or challenged the status quo? Hadn't the creative experience of discovering who she was found its way to her doorstep? Where was her authentic voice?

Leaving the lounge with a shudder, I walked somberly back to my hotel room. The night was over for me. I realized that while it might take decades, burying yourself alive is a distinct option when going about creating a life.

Wisdom Lesson

We must keep our dreams alive.

Our dreams require loyalty, and they need a voice to give them life. We can spend years and years silencing ourselves, not even acknowledging that we *have* a dream. Fear of being fabulous, fear of growth, fear of change, and fear of making others uncomfortable will, in time, result in our drying up and dying to ourselves. At some point, we will turn around and wonder where our lives went.

Silencing our voices really takes a toll. When we are young we can get away with a lot. We have pizzazz on our side and easily trick ourselves into thinking there is plenty of time to go after our dreams. A sense of urgency is absent, and we can be lured into the stupor of wondering if it really matters at all? As the years pile on, our dreams can get sidestepped by legitimate distractions. A dispirited habit can set up and, like cement, stay that way for the rest of our lives.

We get preoccupied with babies that need nurturing, people that need loving, parents that need help, birthday presents that need to be purchased, home appliances that need repair, neighbors that need our shoulders to cry on, résumés that need to be written, careers that need constant review and updating, weddings that need to be planned, monthly bills that need to be paid and credit cards that need to be paid off, closets that require purging, friends in need of comforting, endless cups of tea that need brewing, and bathing suits to camouflage our soft bellies need to be found. We get so busy that we barely notice that twenty, thirty, forty, fifty years have disappeared, and we have forgotten what standing for ourselves means.

It might take a few years, but living without a voice will gradually breed a bitter resentment. Deep down, we know when we have sold ourselves short. It can take ten years or fifty years. Make no mistake about it: resentment is a terrible thing. It nips at the heels and begets pursed lips and hardened eyes. Resentment comes from a lonely place of invisibility that never lets the open light of praise be heard. Resentment causes us to hold our breath so we can get through mechanical days. It is not pretty to see, but it is easy to spot in a woman. I have to question the high price of withholding so much. What are the costs to the soul?

Whenever I see it, I want to run over and hold the woman; I want to rock her in my arms and cry with her for all the exhausting work it has taken for her to dampen her dreams. I want to plant wisdom seeds at her feet and help her push past the fallow soil of resistance to change. And then we will both raise our clear voices and say yes to uncovering the wild shaping power of being true to oneself. We will lift our artful voices and make an honest commitment to dare again. Everything has its price, and the price of wearing ageless beauty well costs nothing less than everything. Only you can decide what you will pay.

Aging beautifully depends on telling the truth and keeping a covenant with ourselves to be fully ourselves. Oh, we are going to be so sorry if we never do what we dream of doing. If we never give a dream a chance, we will have to carry remorse into our aging years, and there will be nothing beautiful about it. Some women dream of saving the world while some report that all they want is to dance naked in the garden. The garden, that blessed metaphor for creativity, expansiveness, and growth, stands ready to be planted. I want to tell all the women who have never danced in the garden, "Take off your clothes and dance! Dance your heart out! Dance until the sweat breaks from your brow."

Have compassion for your sisters who are holding their breath waiting for something to land in their laps. Let go. If there is something you dream of doing, do it! Do it now! Create a life ladder filled with meaningful little steps. That is enough.

Think carefully about the dream, however small, you would like to see come true. Write it down. Nothing is too weird, too out there, too ridiculous, or too costly. Let it rip! You have been managing long enough. It's okay if you feel foolish and afraid. It's understandable you might feel that way. No matter how you look at it, now is the time.

You would be wise to ask yourself these questions:

* What will creating my dreams produce?
* What must be overcome if my dream is to become a reality?
* What must be overcome if I am to take myself seriously?

THE SPIRITUAL TASK OF MEETING YOURSELF FULLY

Trust the heart that beats wildly inside you. Trust the nameless pilgrims who have walked in your shoes, women who watched their bodies change too. Trust the witnesses who wait like devoted midwives to usher in a rebirth of the aging woman. Trust that you are where you are in this moment—whole and ready to answer the knock on the door.

One thing is certain. Aging beautifully is yours if you want it.

Trust beauty as a natural state of being, and trust aging because it is in the right order of things. There is a vastly more powerful and visionary approach to the life stage we have come to know as aging. Have faith in the fourteen-billion-year-old flowering universe and know you are flowering right along with it. That perspective requires a shift in consciousness. It invites us to take a fresh look at a model for growing old and having the courage to embrace it. When we can appreciate aging from a developmental model, it becomes less something to fear than as a salutation to the human tapestry of transformation.

Keep going is a posture to take as our faces and bodies change. With "cures" for aging growing by the day, we are told to do everything in our power to turn the clock back. I have no trouble with creams and lifts. But I do have trouble with not being proud of the life stage called aging. The life stage of aging is the natural evolution of our time on earth. It is the sum of what we think, how we think, and what preoccupies us now. It is written on our faces, in our postures, our strides, our smiles and in our feeling of worth. Our bodies are the uniform for what has preoccupied us all our lives. Keep going. Keep breathing, laughing, wanting, weeping, risking, changing, learning, teaching, dreaming, and loving. To keep going is to sit at the feet of evolution itself.

A good example of keep going is the venerated actress Angela Lansbury, who still performed on Broadway at age eighty-one. She drew people from miles around to witness something so special they were willing to pay almost any price just to get near it. We sat in witness to a life so ageless we wondered if our eyes are playing tricks on us. Most people have an eye for magnificence, and when we actually see it in front of us and realize that magnificence does exist, we are given something to reach for. We *want* to see a life well lived, a person worth emulating, the standard, the best there is. We *want* to behold the quintessence of a life. She means something to us. We love her and stand in awe. There she was, on stage at eighty-one. We are changed just by the sight of her.

Yes, she is old in birthdays and as young as a girl seeking her first love. And if we have any sense, we will make every effort to follow her lead. Not *be* her, but absorb her audacity to thrive. If we asked what kept her going all these years, she might reply: faith in what she loved, consistency, and being true to oneself. She models something else as well. It is something that lives deep within and takes over the heart and floods the mind. It is a force that transcends good intentions, books, years of experience, education, and hours spent on our knees. It is the future calling, a model of the possible and the mystical honey at the front door.

We reach for words, but it is our feelings we should be after. Feelings are real. We have allowed others to hold the Geiger counter of beauty, and millions of us have been hurt in the process. It is time for a new goal, but let's do it with elegance. We do not have to be fueled by anger. We can be fueled by elegance: the least effort for the greatest reward. We will speak with one voice because there is not a woman alive who doesn't believe that aging beautifully isn't a noble goal. And the goal is the transformation of our thinking surrounding aging and beauty. What we are after is what the poets express, music aims for, Bruce Springsteen sings too, athletes spend years achieving, and healers work to find. It is about the human capacity to be powerful and to harness transcendence.

I invite you to embrace a more powerful, visionary view of the aging woman in our twenty-first-century world. It is a view built on wholeheartedness and is directed toward a shift in consciousness surrounding the experience of aging and its ally: beauty.

The Last Prayer

Holy Spirit,
Find me in my desire to age beautifully.
Help me to understand that my
exploration is not self-serving but
represents a genuine desire to
praise all of life, including its end.
Let me be patient with myself as I soar
to new levels of self-appreciation.
Let the sun warm me as I come to
believe I am beautiful and
valuable beyond measure.
Amen.

Acknowledgment

A very special thank you goes to Johnnie Mullin for her technical support and loving interest in bringing this book to press.

Printed in the United States
By Bookmasters